Also by Ben Ratliff

Coltrane: The Story of a Sound

The New York Times Essential Library: Jazz

The
Jazz
Ear

Ben Ratliff

Times Books
Henry Holt and Company
New York

The
Jazz
Ear

Conversations
Over Music

Times Books
Henry Holt and Company, LLC
Publishers since 1866
175 Fifth Avenue
New York, New York 10010
www.henryholt.com

Library of Congress Cataloging-in-Publication Data

Ratliff, Ben.
    The jazz ear: conversations over music / Ben Ratliff. — 1st ed.
        p.   cm.
    Includes bibliographical references and index.
    ISBN-13: 978-0-8050-8146-6
    ISBN-10: 0-8050-8146-1
    1. Jazz musicians — Interviews.   I. Title.
    ML394.R38   2008
    781.65092'2 — dc22   2008010122

First Edition 2008
Designed by Meryl Sussman Levavi
Printed in the United States of America
10 9 8 7 6 5 4 3

Again for K, H, and T

Contents

Contents

Introduction

About fifteen years ago I was spending the afternoon near Times Square at the apartment of Frank Lowe, the onetime free-jazz saxophonist. By this time, though, Lowe was in his middle-aged, Lucky Thompson–worshipping period; all he wanted to do was play murmuring art-deco phrases on his tenor.

Let me briefly describe Frank Lowe. He was a black man with short dreadlocks, tall, skinny, broad-shouldered, and high-cheekboned; streetwise, charming, and slightly bitter. The late 1960s and 1970s had raised some very tough jazz players, who worked through the music's hardest winter of audience neglect. As a result, Lowe had lived in a weird little underground economy for twenty years. He was considered to be on the sentimental and soulful end of the avant-garde, but much of his work still turned away from the mainstream of jazz.

The culture of jazz had changed since he had started performing in the late 1960s. At first he had been an extremist; one of his early records, *Black Beings,* is like drums-and-saxophone scream therapy. He then discovered a way to bring into his work the R & B of his hometown, Memphis, Tennessee, and his music warmed up. He became drawn to the authority and romance of older players in jazz: Lester Young, Coleman Hawkins. By his midforties, when I met him for the first time, I sensed two things: that he knew what kind of saxophonist he wanted to be; and that it might already be too late in his life to get there.

I was young, and he wasn't working much. Both of us had time on our hands. Day turned into night. We went out for Chinese food on Ninth Avenue and came back. He wanted to share some music with me that he'd been listening to.

He dug up two cassettes of records that were new at the time: Abbey Lincoln's *You Gotta Pay the Band* and Joe Henderson's *Lush Life*. The Joe Henderson, particularly, because he wanted to listen to the tracks with Wynton Marsalis playing the trumpet. He'd been paying attention to Marsalis lately, Lowe said. He believed that Marsalis was starting to deliver on his promise.

If you listened to Lowe run down his own potted history, you might make a particular kind of assessment about him. That he rejected current mainstream jazz, wasn't impressed by it anymore, was irritated by its slickness. I was interviewing him, writing about him for a little magazine, and if we had adjourned before just shutting up and listening, the article would have come out differently. The fact is that when we listened to music together, I saw what a shallow caricature that potential assessment was. Lowe had nice ears. I watched his instant reactions to Lincoln and Henderson and Marsalis—certain kinds of phrasing or harmony—and I was understanding him better than I had all day.

We weren't talking about the daily grind anymore, and I saw a great side of him.

One way to interview a musician, I have found, is to talk about subjects that don't really matter, which could include his or her new record. I mean that they "don't matter" if the resulting exchanges end up benefiting a lot of other people besides the musician: the employees and shareholders of the record label, the publicists paid to create an international "conversation," the critics paid to review the record, the secondhand merchants who resell copies on eBay, and finally the operatives of the waste-processing plants who after some years must destroy the remaining, unsellable stock.

But I also mean "don't matter" in terms of the level of commitment or excitement in the conversation. Sometimes a jazz musician will talk to a reporter about his or her own *life* in a way that mostly serves a product or benefits other people; the narratives are practiced and packaged so that readers of the article will pull the trigger and buy a CD. In these cases, the musician might use self-protective or self-aggrandizing language, keeping one eye on the main chance. Or the musician might turn the talk to the conceptual ideas behind each track on the new album.

The question, then, is how to bump a great jazz musician out of a mercantile or defensive mode. It can help if the musician's own work isn't at stake. And it can help if a CD player is nearby.

Why would musicians ever talk to a journalist about what really matters if it's not in line with their professional interests? I don't know. I try not to think about that. But none of my conversations over music have been unpleasant. Usually they are almost ecstatic. We get into it gently. I would never want to start a conversation with a musician—except Ornette Coleman—by turning on a recorder and asking: say, what is music for? In many cases I don't really know the musician socially, so we need some kind of emulsion; this is what music does.

Listening with someone else is an intimate act, because music reveals itself by degrees. With a few people who have particularly high manners—for instance, Hank Jones and Dianne Reeves—sometimes, at first, it can feel a little too close. It's a process of surprises and, because these are not visual surprises, the listeners tend to look at each other, determining whether they both understood what has just happened. It prompts confessions that cut against the grain of journalism and its system of cultural classification, the horrid little grid boxes ("postbop," "avant-garde," "romantic," "cool," "neoclassical," and all their assumed traits of art or character) into which musicians are installed by their critics.

A lot of jazz musicians do not really like to take apart a work of jazz music and consider it from a distance, as a flattened whole: the mechanics of a groove, the logic of the composition, the symmetries of its structure. And many—perhaps even most—great jazz musicians are fairly uninterested in the history of jazz criticism, the historical consensus of written opinion about certain players or bands or records. Most of them believe that all this is somehow hostile to their enterprise. It's playing with a good thing, pushing back against a magic concordance.

On the other hand, jazz musicians love to hear really well-played jazz *as it moves along*; they react and shout and laugh to it. Some of the musicians in this book have been trained academically, while others have been trained on bandstands. But they all make up their own terms of music criticism, which is one of the reasons that I get so much out of listening with them. The drummer Paul Motian shrinks from any kind of musical analysis, but loves it when the drummer in a band honors the melody and structure of a song. The guitarist Pat Metheny has no problem with analysis—he has a precise and empirical mind—yet he looks for a very unprecise quality in music, what he calls *glue*. The pianist Bebo Valdés thinks about making technical ambition shine through a modern-sounding arrangement. The singer Dianne Reeves is fascinated by moments of transparency in music, when a band or a performer brings the listener into its own closed loop, and the words take on an almost embarrassing directness.

Don't get me wrong; "making up their own terms" is not some sort of metaphor for improvisation. These musicians don't invent these concerns on the spot; they cultivate them over many years, as an outgrowth of their larger philosophy and cast of mind. They are true and personal and deep concerns. And if these encounters sometimes get away from music and spill over into character profiles, that's intentional. I can't get inside anyone's head. (I am usually forbidden to; constructions like "he thought" or "she intended" are discouraged by the *New York Times*'s stylebook.) But I can try to reconcile the things each person said with the things he or she heard and triangulate a point of view.

My conversations occurred between December 2004 and March 2007. We ran them as a series in the paper and called it "Listening With." I approached musicians who I thought were all either important elders in the music or making excellent work. (They also had to be people with whom I knew I would enjoy spending a long afternoon.) I asked each one to come up with a list of five or six pieces of music that he or she would like to listen to with me. Any kind of music was fine, as long as that musician hadn't taken part in it. We spoke on the phone for a while to talk through any fears or inhibitions (there were many); then we got together, preferably and usually at the musician's home, and spent three or four hours together. I asked simple questions and tried to let the ideas rise up on their own. It makes me smile to notice how, among all these hearings, certain people and notions make repeat appearances: Baby Dodds's philosophy of how to play drums in a jazz band; Art Tatum's keyboard runs; "inevitability" in a piece of jazz; the examples and never-ending lessons of Max Roach, Wayne Shorter, Charlie Parker, and Sonny Rollins.

There are various precedents for this kind of writing. One is the "blindfold test," which Leonard Feather started practicing in *Down Beat* in 1946 and which has remained a regular feature of the magazine. He really did use blindfolds, at least at first, and played tracks to a musician for an attempt at identification and then an instant reaction. There was an element in this of catching musicians up short, like making them taste wine with blanked-out labels. It was meant to start a purer way of talking about music, without the usual prejudices and cliquishness, and sometimes it did. But I'm not interested in fooling people or exposing their weaknesses. Within reason, I insisted that the musicians choose the music. I was looking for the ongoing experience of being with them as we listened to something that they knew well.

The other precedent—closer to what I have done here—was that of the visual-art critic walking through a museum with an artist and documenting the resulting conversation. Michael Kimmelman at the *Times* did this very elegantly in the mid-1990s for his book *Portraits*. He recorded several different reactions: the artist's reaction to the work itself, along with his or her built-in feelings about spaces in which to experience art and how best to contemplate it. My conversations tended to be looser by necessity. We weren't looking at a fixed object or image; obviously, music keeps wriggling on, and you try to keep up with it. Often the musician and I would listen to a piece of music again, to catch something interesting that had moved too quickly the first time around. We usually weren't in neutral locations; most of the time they listened the way they normally listened, through their own equipment, with their own lives poking in: phones ringing, babies crying, dogs barking.

What really matters, I think, is how musicians hear. What are the things they notice? What are their criteria for excellence? What makes them react involuntarily? The answers indicate what a musician values in music, which connects to what a musician believes music is for in the first place. And that is the big thing, the big question, from which all small questions descend.

The
Jazz
Ear

Behold, the Sea!

Wayne Shorter

There's a story I like about Wayne Shorter. It's told in *Foot-prints,* Michelle Mercer's biography of Shorter, a book that folded in his voice and which may have to serve as his autobiography, unless he writes a proper one. It is told by Hal Miller, a jazz historian who sometimes traveled on tour with Weather Report, the band Shorter played saxophone with from 1971 to 1985.

"I remember once I asked Wayne for the time," Miller told Mercer. "He started talking to me about the cosmos and how time is relative." Miller and Shorter were waiting somewhere—an airport, a train station, a hotel. The band's keyboardist, Joe Zawinul, who took charge of such matters as what the road crew was supposed to do and when, set Miller straight. "You don't ask Wayne shit like that," he snapped. "It's 7:06 p.m."

I have had similar conversations with Shorter over the years. Not long after I read that book, I got in touch with him, hoping we could listen to some music that he admired, as a way into having a conversation about music and, ultimately, about his own work. I figured that the exchange might be one ballooned 7:06 p.m., but I also figured that as long as we were listening to the same music at the same time, the conversation wouldn't break down. After he finished a European tour with his quartet, we got together on a December afternoon at his home in Aventura, Florida, less a town than a thicket of tall condominium towers near the ocean.

Since he went back on the road with an acoustic jazz quartet in 2001, after an extended period of fits and starts following the breakup of Weather Report, Shorter's shows have built up a consensus of awe seldom encountered in the splintered world of jazz. He has been playing his own compositions—from his days with the mid-1960s Miles Davis Quintet to pieces from later solo records—and establishing that there is a way of writing tunes for a hard-core jazz group that are not codified by style as soon as they hit the music paper. The pieces are open-ended, a function of his temperament, as a few hours in his company makes clear.

Shorter, born and raised in Newark, New Jersey, has a cast of mind that makes his jazz almost zenlike. His songs are succinct, clever, sometimes even cute, but they also pose unanswerable questions. Many of his songs from the mid-1960s, when he was turning out one small masterpiece after another—"Fall," "Limbo," "Nefertiti," "Et Cetera," "Orbits"—are dressed in odd phrase lengths and rarefied harmonies. They can seem too fragile to be bruised in a nightclub.

A test of jazz musicians and composers is whether their writing can succeed outside their own creators' preferred context: a trio, a quartet, a big band, or whatever. Wayne Shorter's "Footprints," "Speak No Evil," and "Infant Eyes" have been common standards for a long time now, played in many different types of bands, with other compositions of his approaching that level. Likewise, it's not just with his quartet that he can slay audiences. I once saw him walk on stage for a single solo, on a version of Antonio Carlos Jobim's "Dindi," with the singer Flora Purim. It was spectacular, a grainy, evocative, playful thing that kept striking earthy and far-out patterns. He had just turned seventy-one at the time and gave no indication of having decided that he could rely on a boiler-plate version of his own sound.

Standing at the windows of his apartment tower, Shorter pointed out the nearby buildings where Whitney Houston and Sophia Loren lived, then showed me a catalog of new work by his wife's cousin, a sculptor from São Paulo. (In 1999 he married Carolina dos Santos, a singer and actress, his third wife.) Finally, he produced a box set of music by Ralph Vaughan Williams, conducted by Sir Adrian Boult. "I got something good for you," he said.

I had been expecting classical music. Some of his recent works have been rearrangements, for orchestra and jazz quartet, of Villa-Lobos and Sibelius. I thought he might pick Stravinsky, the bebopper's idol. But this choice made sense, too; the English composer Vaughan Williams, directly or indirectly, influenced many postwar film composers, and if there's one artistic stimulus that Shorter always seems open to, it is the movies.

Small and cheery, dressed in I'm-not-going-outside-today clothes and bedroom slippers, he spent some time struggling to set the Krell home-theater preamp so that it could play a CD. I was forming a suspicion that he didn't listen to music much.

"Hey, man, the Krell. You ever see the movie *Forbidden Planet?*" he asked. "There was this planet full of people called the Krells. And nobody had been there from Earth—the explorers from

Earth didn't see anybody when they arrived. But they all went to sleep one night in their spacecraft, and you hear the first sound of special effects that really came to the fore in movies—this *chrrmmm! Chroooom!* And you see the ground that's been depressed by huge footprints, not human . . ."

He first chose the opening of Vaughan Williams's Symphony no. 1: "A Song for All Seas, All Ships," composed in 1910, with orchestra and choir singing lines taken from a poem by Walt Whitman. After the fanfare, twenty seconds into the piece, as the strings begin to rise dramatically, Shorter smiled. "Life, that's what he's saying," he said. "It's a metaphor for life."

It is superhero music. (Shorter, who is not cagey about his enthusiasms, wore a blue Superman T-shirt that day.) "Behold," the chorus sang out again, "the sea!" The cymbals crashed, illustrating a wave, and then the tempo fell off, the sound dispersing like spray.

"I like that," he said. "It's almost saying, 'Look at your life.' If anybody wants to commit suicide, just take a look at your life. Look in the mirror. Because we are the ship." The brass lines grew denser. "I like that, the little line in the bass going down, the contrary motion. It's like describing a thing that you don't need to worry about. It's like, life should be *awesome*. The lyrics are saying something else, but there are some things that lyrics cannot express." The chorus came back again. "Power!" he said, grinning.

"I only heard this piece eight or nine months ago," he explained, motioning to the box set we were listening to, which he had just unwrapped. "But Ralph Vaughan Williams, I've been tracking him since I was about sixteen or seventeen. I used to listen to a program called *New Ideas in Music*, which came on every Saturday at noon on the radio."

Shorter's mother worked for a furrier in Newark. His father was a welder at the Singer sewing machine factory in Elizabeth, New Jersey. As *Footprints* tells it, Shorter and his older brother, Alan, cultivated radical artistic temperaments, encouraged by their parents. By their teenage years, they had formed their own clique of surrealists.

In 1950, when bebop was still largely a thing of mystery to high schoolers outside of the big city, Wayne and Alan performed Dizzy Gillespie tunes at a school concert, dressed in wrinkled suits and galoshes, pretending to sight-read the newspapers on their music stands. In those days, Shorter painted the words "Mr. Weird" on his saxophone case, and he still could; he speaks in disjunctive bursts, frequently lapsing into silence halfway through a sentence. Sometimes you think you get his meaning, and then, sadly, you discover you couldn't have been following a colder trail.

But in many ways his youth was quite normal for the 1940s: filled with radio, comic books, and movies. His study, where he composes at a small desk with score paper, pen, Wite-Out, and a half-size keyboard, is filled not with music CDs but with videocassettes and laser discs: Dean Martin celebrity roasts, *For the Love of Ivy*, *The Bad Seed*, *Quilombo*, *The Ugly American*.

Next Shorter wanted me to hear Vaughan Williams's "The Lark Ascending," which he performed both in the concert band at New York University, when he was a music education major, and then in the army band during his service from 1956 to 1958. (He was stationed in Fort Dix, New Jersey.) But as I found out later when I bought my own copy of the box set, there is a manufacturer's mistake in the track numbering for that particular disc. We couldn't find the "Lark," so we settled instead for "Norfolk Rhapsody no. 1," composed in 1905 and 1906, which he also likes.

A clarinet bubbles up with a tendril of a line, following a violin; they are complementary versions of the same melodic idea. The strings slither quietly underneath. As the clarinet and violin gestures keep repeating, a tense feeling of stasis begins to take over. "*Happening*," he muttered. Later in the piece, when further iterations of the line move higher, through different keys, it reminded me a little bit of his own "Nefertiti," from 1967, with the Miles Davis Quintet, whose long melody tensely runs a five-note pattern through different chords, without a solo ever actually coming to pass.

"We're gonna get into some Symphony no. 4 next," he said. He put on the opening of the first movement, a dramatically brooding thing. "I guess some of the early writers of movie music got this," he said, as a noirish romantic theme emerged from a thunder of kettle drums and bass trombones. "Like the John Williams music in the film of Hemingway's *The Killers*."

I asked if he particularly likes music that suggests something about human temperament. "Yeah!" he said, brightly. "And also *going* . . . ," he said, making a pushing-out-into-the-universe gesture. "You know, the unknown! I'll put on the scherzo."

The gremlin music of the scherzo heated up, turning into a passage of gnarled, menacing little three-note jabs-and-parries in the strings and brass. "You know that Coltrane got some of that stuff," he said, mimicking hands-on-the-saxophone. "*Duhdeluh* . . . *duhdeluh duhdeluh* . . ."

Shorter and Coltrane were close; he was Coltrane's first significant long-term replacement in Miles Davis's band, and had been very early to understand and absorb Coltrane's improvisational style. (He saw Coltrane with the Davis band, in Washington, D.C., probably in November 1955; David Amram, the French horn player, remembered meeting Shorter that winter at the 125 Club in Harlem and hearing his raves about Coltrane.) Shorter chose to emulate where he thought Coltrane was going rather than where he had just been, and they ended up in very different places, Shorter with epigrams and Coltrane with epics.

"It's like something from a movie! 'Titanius! Agamemnon!'" he cried, assuming an actorly baritone. "It's like Errol Flynn fighting with Basil Rathbone: *chik-chik-chik*! This is happening," he said.

The music changed again, becoming less agitated and more hopeful. "And here's the seafaring stuff, the sailor thing . . . or it could be astronauts. *We need a large vehicle to get beyond this gravity and away from our decadent thinking*," Shorter intoned.

He still wanted to play me more. He found the dark, almost violent Symphony no. 6—Vaughan Williams finished it not long after the bombing of Hiroshima—and went right to the scherzo. "There's a little Stravinsky in there," he said, "but that's all right; the pagan thing." Then, about two minutes in, a tenor saxophonist enters, as the music scales down to a trio and shifts harmonically, with a new melody. "Dig him!" Shorter crowed. "He came right out of the wall! I like how that whole thing came out from the side."

In the mid-1970s Shorter moved to Los Angeles and became involved with Soka Gakkai International, the American-based group associated with Nichiren Buddhism—the sect that chants *Nam-myoho-renge-kyo*. (His commitment to the practice shortly followed that of Herbie Hancock, his partner in the Miles Davis group of the 1960s.) The philosophy of Nichiren Buddhism—

particularly the idea of "the eternal self," and taking responsibility for one's life—serves as the root of most of his big ideas.

"It comes down to people," he said, "people awakening to this whole thing called eternity. And not thinking that 'you gotta do it now,' and 'if you don't do it now you'll never do it because you only live once.' If you think you only live once, you're gonna have war. You're gonna have bank robbers. They're not gonna study or care about anyone else. It's like Enron: 'we need a quick way to get a house in the Bahamas.' When a person gets rich, they've got half of something. But the half gets confused with the whole. If I thought that 106 South Street was the whole world—which I did, it was the house where I grew up—then I was an isolationist. If I'm still thinking that way right now, I'm a hell of an isolationist.

"People talk about connecting all the dots. But there have been experts at *disconnecting* dots. You know, the dogmatic thing is to say, the only time you're gonna have to redeem yourself is now. And if it's too late, you're gonna go to *hell*"—he made a severe face—"or, heb'n," he said, putting on a dumb, credulous voice. "I don't believe that shit."

He went on. "It's no great mystery about why things are the way they are. Doubt, denial, fear, trepidation reinforce the artificial barriers to the real, the barriers that keep us from going into the real adventure of eternity. If you don't believe we have eternity, it doesn't matter; it's there. You'll never be bored. I think you'll always be you, and I'll always be me. When you say 'what is life?'— well, life is the one time you have an eternal adventure." He looked pleased. "Sounds like a contradiction. *The one time you have an eternal adventure.* I like that! It rubs against itself; it makes sparks. To me those sparks are fuel."

* * *

"I don't really listen to music," he said later in the day, not to my great surprise. "I listen to music when I'm making a record; I listen to what we're doing. But I don't listen to music because there are not that many close sequences of chance-taking over any period of time. You have to wait until someone has the courage to come and jump into deep water. You have to wait a long time for a Marlon Brando. You have to wait a long time for a good close encounter of the third, or fifth, or tenth kind. I have *Steven Spielberg Presents: Taken*, the miniseries," he said, excitedly, "and it's still in its cellophane. I'm waiting to match that kind of time, to see it all at once, when it can really be appreciated—not just to see it because I have it."

What has he heard in passing lately that he liked?

"Occasionally I will hear twenty seconds of something in a film score," he allowed. "I liked John Williams's opening music to *Catch Me If You Can*. I like the depth and breadth of sound that he can get to reflect the vastness of something—of space. I like James Newton Howard, too, his way of not always seeming like he has another film to score. James Horner, I liked his score for *Glory*, with the Harlem Boys' Choir. I like Bernard Herrmann's score to *One Million BC*, the movie with Victor Mature and Carole Landis—she committed suicide . . ."

But his comment as we listened to Symphony no. 4 had me curious. Did Coltrane listen to Vaughan Williams, too? "I don't know," he said. "But like Charlie Parker, he probably listened to everything." Did Shorter ever meet Parker? "No, but I saw him about five times. I sneaked into a theater one time, when I was about fifteen. The fire escape, back of the theater, mezzanine, and there was Bird with strings, playing 'Laura.' I liked Bird with strings. The word was like, it's a novelty, it won't last, but Bird really wanted to work with the orchestra."

Shorter said he had been looking at semiretirement, which meant less time on the road and more time thinking about composing music that would contain only a little of his playing—"not all over the place, just where it counts." One such piece is "Aurora Leigh," a composition which he started when he was eighteen and at NYU, named after an Elizabeth Barrett Browning poem; he said he might bring it to David Robertson, the principal conductor of the St. Louis Symphony Orchestra, who wanted to work with him. Recently, he said, he had begun to work with the soprano Renée Fleming, writing original music for her to sing.

"When I listen to music, I'm not thinking about the workshop aspect of it," he said. "'Oh, that sound goes good against that one.' *Boring.* But, you know, Elgar, who wrote something about people that he knew, characters he knew?" (He was describing *The Enigma Variations.*) "Each theme was antiphonal. You say, 'Describe this person in music,' and he'd do it, whether the person was rotund or skinny.

"I need to find out more about other people's cultures, with the time I have left," Shorter said, jumping over a conversational hedgerow. "Because when I'm writing something that sounds like my music . . . well, not *my music*, I don't possess music—but when they say 'Wayne Shorter's playing those snake lines,' I should take that willingness to do that, that desire I have to do that, and extend it to the desire to find out more about what is not easy to follow, what is difficult to follow in someone else's life."

I asked if he would like to hear one more piece of music.

"Do you think that would enhance what you're writing, so people could hear through your words?" he asked, without really waiting for an answer. "I used to think, what the hell is music for?" Shorter mused. "Like, what is law for? Is it for immediate checks and balances and controls? But then what is it *really* for? And music—is it an aphrodisiac, a convincer, a manacle? You know, '*I gotta have my rhythm and blues, man . . .*'"

What if I were to ask him if there was some piece of music, or some kind of music, that had altered his life in a positive way? How would he reply to that?

"Actually, music hasn't changed my life; it's the other way around. Somebody asked me that once, a young guy in Spain. He said, 'What has life taught you?' I said, wait a minute, think of it this way: what can you teach life?" He talked further about this "human revolutionary process," then concluded: "For me to be aware of something that has great value, I change my life."

I tried rephrasing the question. Is there music that embodies a value for which you would change your life?

"See, to me, the sound of music is neutral," he returned. "What I do is arrange the dialogue, the musical dialogue, in a way that has not been spoken to me before."

Does he often hear a piece of music and think that he hears himself represented in it?

"Oh, yeah. I used to play all kinds of records, and I'd get my clarinet and get right in it. One thing I liked about Charlie Parker: he'd play that song 'South of the Border, Down Mexico Way.' That's a *nice* song. One of Gene Autry's hit songs. Nothing complicated, but I like it."

Set List

Ralph Vaughan Williams, *The Complete Symphonies*, conducted by Sir Adrian Boult, EMI boxed set, recorded 1967–75.

2

Street Music

Pat Metheny

It was one of the coldest days of the winter and the guitarist Pat Metheny was only a few minutes late, but he had called ahead. When he arrived at our meeting place, a small recording studio within Right Track Studios on West Forty-eighth Street in New York City, he arranged his things—including some musical scores—on the couch and sat down in a swivel chair before a ninety-six-channel console. Metheny grew up in the rural Midwest but seems Californian; he has the inner glow. He had no socks on and looked comfortable.

"Basically, it's impossible," he said flatly, and smiled. "My taste, my general connection to music, I mean, even now, I think it just *can't be done*."

I had proposed that we listen together to a few pieces of music that affected him strongly. It could be any music: not desert-island endorsements or a strict autobiography of influence; the point was to talk about how music works and how he hears it. Metheny took the challenge seriously.

"For me to say I'm going to build a case that describes something, under the guise of three songs, it actually shuts me down a little bit," he said, seeming pained. "The whole idea of style and genre is actually something I've willfully resisted from the very early stage. So if I pick this and then I pick that, it creates these two pillars. But I think I know what you're looking for, which has nothing to do with what I'm talking about."

He began to warm up. "I don't think too much about stuff like this, and it's been kind of a musical psychoanalysis. Most musicians are occasionally asked to put together their ten favorite albums, but you're looking for the *undercurrents* to it all."

"You've got it perfectly," I said.

He took a CD-R out of its case, onto which he had burned six pieces of music. "Well, then let's start with Sonny Rollins and Paul Bley."

Dealing with great jazz improvisers is often dealing with masters of certainty: people who for most of their lives have been trusting their impulses to make things up on the spot. Metheny—fifty years old at the time of our meeting, in 2005—extends that certainty to talking, exhaustively, about music, both in specifics and at a conceptual or historical remove.

He is ecumenical and opinionated, practical and quite idealistic, a cheery defender of his own causes. Although he is a jazz musician at the core and is generally thought of as such, he does not believe his purpose in life is to further the cause of the guitar in jazz, or even of jazz itself.

On the telephone a few days before, I had asked him whether

he'd be talking about a lot of guitarists. "The guitar for me is a translation device," he said by way of an answer. "It's not a goal. And in some ways jazz isn't a destination for me. For me, jazz is a vehicle that takes you to the true destination—a musical one that describes all kinds of stuff about the human condition and the way music works."

Growing up in Missouri, Metheny developed his certainty as a high-school-age professional in Kansas City. In 1975, when he was twenty-one, he made his first album, *Bright Size Life*, with a trio including Jaco Pastorius on bass and Bob Moses on drums, and started to bring about a change within jazz—a compositional one, really, that affected all kinds of instrumentalists, not just guitarists. The record introduced a lyrical strain in the music that didn't come from the blues or old popular standards; he was not aggressively overplaying, as many jazz-into-rock guitarists were at the time, and he suggested new areas of harmony that had not yet flooded American jazz pedagogy, but soon would.

A few years later he formed the Pat Metheny Group and has kept some form of it together since 1977, playing music that is melodically rich, harmonically advanced, besotted with the possibilities of effects and recording technology, and often kind of glossily pretty. That prettiness—and the adaptations he has made to the sound of the guitar, especially the guitar synthesizer, with its limpid, brasslike sound—has been insurmountable for many people who prefer their jazz based in the rudiments of swing and blues, and in acoustic sounds. But his audience has never abated.

Pay attention to his work, and he will eventually get around to whatever it is you like, whether it be *Question and Answer*, a record of tough, imaginative postbebop and post-Coltrane playing with the bassist Dave Holland and the drummer Roy Haynes; his pop-fusion melodies with the Pat Metheny Group; his solo acoustic records; or separate collaborations with his heroes Ornette Coleman and Jim Hall and Derek Bailey. It is a weirdly wide aesthetic swath.

The Pat Metheny Group reshaped itself in the last decade, bringing in some of jazz's best young players, including the trumpeter Cuong Vu, the harmonica player Grégoire Maret, and the drummer Antonio Sanchez, for a 2005 record, *The Way Up*. In general, Metheny made curious moves in the 1990s and the first decade of the twenty-first century: a very strummy solo record for baritone acoustic guitar, some duet records with the pianist Brad Mehldau, some work in a trio with the bassist Christian McBride and Sanchez, again. For young musicians, working with Metheny is no small thing. He has a worldwide audience, and a tour with him means a good financial year. But you often come away with the sense that Metheny gets even a bigger charge out of it than they do. It's more necessary information, more pleasurable study.

The Way Up is Metheny's most ambitious work. Ascending melodic passages keep driving through it, and though certain themes return after long stretches, this is not short-form music, like most jazz. It is a sixty-eight-minute-long, through-composed suite, redolent in parts of Steve Reich, and its score has no repeat signs.

If you knew Metheny only from hearing his work played on smooth-jazz stations in the 1980s, records like this would be a surprise. But then you have to remember that over the past decade or so he has been first in line to disparage smooth jazz as anti-intellectual snake oil. (His fulminating criticism of Kenny G.'s posthumous duet with Louis Armstrong in the song "What a Wonderful World," posted on his Web site, became probably the most widely read piece of jazz criticism in the year 2000.) More to the point, he seems always to be looking to surprise you. What he appreciates in music, beyond a certain requisite level of technique, is very difficult to quantify.

He is broad-minded—and among established jazz musicians, this is a rarer condition than many think. He has the enthusiasm and energy of someone much younger, and surprising amounts of both seem purely focused toward making music. On his site, he answers his devotees' questions about other musicians in jazz, rock, and classical music with testimonials that he has checked them out, rigorously citing particular concerts or records. "Sure . . . ," goes a typical Metheny response to a question about a progressive-rock guitarist, "I have been following Buckethead's thing closely since he came on the scene about 10 years ago now . . ."

Elsewhere a fan asks whether Metheny is a wine or beer drinker—and if so, which regions, microbrews, and so forth, does he favor. A reasonable question for a man of such discernment. Metheny's answer seemed to reveal something about his stamina, his focus, and his seriousness: "weirdly, i have never tasted wine or beer. no special reason, just never interested in it."

* * *

In 1963, Sonny Rollins made a fascinatingly tense record with his saxophone-playing role model, Coleman Hawkins. *Sonny Meets Hawk!* had an almost transparently psychological subtext: Rollins wasn't trying to outsmart his aesthetic idol so much as to be very, very himself, with all possible eccentricities, in the face of Hawkins's magnificence.

"He was a young guy at the time," Metheny marveled, listening to Rollins's emphatic, darting lines in "All the Things You Are," harmonically at odds with Hawkins's, on the opening chorus. "That feeling is such a great feeling—like 'I can play *anything*, and it's all good.' Not to analyze it, but Hawk was kind of like his father. And it's like Sonny's saying, 'yeah, *but* . . .'"

What especially attracts Metheny to the track, though, is Paul Bley's piano solo. It is made of elegant, flowing phrases that move in and around the tonality and the melody of the song; it builds momentum and becomes carried away with itself. Metheny calls the solo "the shot heard 'round the world," in terms of its aftereffects in subsequent jazz, especially through Keith Jarrett.

"I think maybe we should just stop there," he said at the end of Bley's solo. He had a point to make about this song; he wasn't going to get distracted with more minutes of it.

It seems to me, I said, that Bley was playing phrases that were very articulate and coherent within themselves. They sometimes clashed with the guiding harmony of the piece. But what he was doing sounded inevitable.

He looked pleased. "You used a word that describes everything that I've brought in today, which is *inevitability*. And the inevitability that I respond to is less on the cultural scale than on the melodic scale. The thing about that solo for me is: there's a certain kind of elusive and very mysterious *groove* that connects things melodically and rhythmically, that offers a certain kind of resonance or truth or power that you can't really quantify." He backed up. "If you talk about what is a great tune or a great solo, there are all these things you can quantify. There's a million things we could talk about here, harmonically, that are actually fairly specific. We could go to the piano and break them down. I think that has to do with this area you're talking about, of clashing. Rhythmically, there's also some really amazing stuff going on there.

"His relationship to time," Metheny went on, "is the best sort of pushing and pulling, wrestling with it and at the same time, phrase by phrase, making these interesting connections between bass and drums, making it seem like it's a little bit on top, and then now it's a little bit behind." (He held an index finger straight up, and moved it slightly to the right and left, like a bubble in a carpenter's level.)

"But there's also this X factor," he continued. "It's the sense of each thing leading very naturally to the next thing. He's letting each idea go to its own natural conclusion. He's reconciling that with a form, of course, that we all know very well. And he's following the harmony, but he's not. It just feels like, 'why didn't anybody else do that before?' And it's still being absorbed, I think."

There is a plainspokenness, a natural folk feeling, to Bley's lines and his harmony, I added. Is the idea of "inevitability" related to that?

"Well, for me," he answered, "let's keep jazz as folk music. Let's not make jazz classical music. Let's keep it as street music, as people's everyday-life music. Let's see jazz musicians continue to use the materials, the tools, the spirit of the actual time that they're living in as what they build their lives as musicians around." In vernacular art, he said, he saw an inevitability.

"It's a cliché, but it's such a valuable one: something that is the most personal becomes the most universal."

Next we heard "Seven Steps to Heaven," performed live by the Miles Davis Quintet—including Herbie Hancock, George Coleman, Ron Carter, and Tony Williams—in 1964. It is fast and confident, even in its improvised coda; Williams's drum solo crackles like gunfire, and Davis's solo is coolly imperious.

"This is the first record I ever got," Metheny said, as a prologue. "I got this when I was eleven. My older brother Mike, who's a great trumpet player, had a couple of friends who were starting to get interested in jazz. He brought this record home. I always hear 'jazz is something you really have to learn about, and you develop a taste for it, and da da da,' that whole rap. But for me, as an eleven-year-old, within thirty seconds of hearing this record"—he snapped his fingers—"I was down for life."

We listened to it silently. "They were really rushing," he commented when it finished. "I know Herbie really well and I knew Tony very well too, and I've talked with them about what was actually going down that night. They thought it was one of the worst gigs they'd ever done. But I was listening to Tony here. The same way the Bley thing opened up this universe—well, Tony too. It's such an incredibly fresh way of thinking of time. It sums up so much of what that period was. The world was about to shift."

He redirected himself. "But what I was going to talk about is Miles's solo."

Metheny is absolutely heroic to contemporary jazz students—as a prodigy, an inveterate learner, a language changer, and a bridge between different styles of music. (By his list of recordings and performances, he links in many directions. Here are some of the musicians who are separated from him by one degree: Roy Haynes, Charlie Haden, Derek Bailey, Jaco Pastorius, Joni Mitchell, Jim Hall, David Bowie, Milton Nascimento, Brad Mehldau, Ornette Coleman, Abbey Lincoln.)

He sees creeping academicism in jazz as a calamitous area. Whenever his conversation turns to jazz pedagogy, or when he finds himself speaking to jazz students in a clinic or a lecture, he becomes very precise.

"This is the kind of tune that, you know, if we go down to the New School now"—referring to the institution in New York City that's been particularly successful at producing young jazz musicians—"we're going to find fifty guys who can just eat this tune alive, in the way that the jazz education movement has evolved toward." (He meant that they could play it precisely and even speedily, to the point of glibness.) "But there is not *one second* in what Miles plays in his solo that has anything to do with any of that. It's this completely invented language that happens to line up perfectly with all the things we now have quantified in jazz in terms of its language and grammar. It wasn't quantified then, as it is now, that if you see *this* kind of chord, you're going to play *this* set of notes.

"We could say the same thing about Coleman Hawkins. You know, they weren't thinking in those terms. You kind of had to make up your own system." (What Metheny wasn't saying is that he made up his own.)

"The thing about Miles, of course, is that he played a lot of the same stuff a lot of the time, while everything around him kept changing," Metheny noted. "But on the other hand, this is not an easy tune. It's not like playing on a blues. It moves around a couple of keys, then a bridge, does a weird move that you've got to deal with. He deals with it in such an abstract, hip way. It's melody, and it has this whole thing of *glue*—the way ideas are connected with other ideas on a phrase-by-phrase basis."

Davis had to slow down his imagination to a much calmer tempo than the song's, I suggested, to imply all that swing in each note and phrase.

Metheny took a deep breath. "Yeah. You know, that word *swing* is almost a political buzzword. To me, in the language I'm using here, that's the glue I'm talking about. The connection of ideas. To me, the jazz education movement is really interested in quantifying these things, even on a sort of political-cultural spectrum. But to me what's beautiful about this is that it's prequantification. The most abstract thing in the world can swing, in terms of this glue quotient. Cecil Taylor, Derek Bailey—to me, this stuff has got unbelievable glue."

For another reference, I mentioned the Albert Ayler records with Gary Peacock and Sunny Murray—those whirling, intuitively coordinated early examples of free jazz. They just inherently work. You can call it abstract music, but the musicians know the language and the dimensions they're going to fill, and it's very graceful.

"Absolutely. It's how things are connected. It doesn't matter if we're going to talk about Bach or Miles or Stevie Wonder or the Beatles. What I love is the stuff that makes the music connect," he said. "But there's another way that music connects: with who the person is, the time he's living in, how he's able to manifest a sound that represents all that. To me, that's swing, and it doesn't have anything to do with jazz." (His midwestern accent renders the word "jee-azz.")

"Swing is kind of this *quality*? It exists in human interaction. In the way somebody talks and moves. I find its resonance in architecture, and literature."

Acting?

"Yeah, acting. And refrigerator repair."

Metheny's popularity jumped to a much higher level in 1979 with his record *American Garage*. For about fifteen years thereafter, he had no roots other than an apartment in Boston that kept the rain off of his answering machine. Now he lives in New York City, in an Upper West Side high-rise, with his French-Moroccan wife, Latifa, and two young sons, Jeff Kaiis and Nicolas Djakeem.

For a few years during that period he spent a lot of time in Brazil and got to know Antonio Carlos Jobim before the great composer died in 1994. (The influence of Brazilian music on Metheny, rather than the reverse, is an often-disputed point.) Metheny wanted to hear "Passarim," a condensed three-and-a-half-minute piece from Jobim's last album, whose words protest environmental pollution; it is the title track of a CD released in both English and Portuguese, and we listened to the Portuguese version.

Metheny smiled as the music started. "It's so much more than a tune," he began. "This is really like *composition*. Especially that little bit." He backed up the disc to where the chorus of female voices, many of them members of Jobim's family, repeated lines over a descending harmonic motion.

Jobim's catarrhal voice reentered. "See, you could call this part the bridge, except that it keeps spinning off into this other stuff, kind of like in 'Desafinado.' It should end there, after he's finished, but it doesn't, and it goes into this whole other thing. Then it keeps modulating into these different keys." The music suddenly shifted from bossa to waltz time. "This is *so advanced*. The beauty of the harmony—major triads moving down throughout this whole thing, with different kinds of voices. Plus, all that glue, melodic glue; it never stops, from the first note to the end. Where are we now? We're almost two minutes into the track, where nothing has repeated yet. I mean, that's advanced the way Paul Bley is advanced. There's a connection there."

It works because Jobim's ideas are complete within themselves, I suggested. Does he will them to fit together, regardless of traditional ideas of structure?

"Yeah. It's like when you first wake up in the morning and you don't really think about what you're doing, and maybe you write your best stuff. You're not in the way. When talking about writing, I often use the analogy of archaeology. There are these great tunes all around. Your skill as a musician allows you to pick them out without breaking them."

After Paul Bley, his supernova—and then issues of rhythm, melody, harmony, and extended composition—Metheny wanted to talk about touch. He put on Bach's Fugue no. 22 in B-flat Minor, from the pianist Glenn Gould's 1965 recording of Bach's *Well-Tempered Clavier,* Book 1, and read along from the score.

"B-flat minor, the saddest of all keys," Metheny muttered, at the end.

He began talking at the same speed as before—brisk, insistent—but much lower and more quietly. "There's a billion things to talk about here, but the main reason I picked this was the way he was able to invoke this almost lyrical, vocal, singing quality from an instrument that doesn't involve breath. And, of course, when you play an instrument, one of the real challenges is to somehow conjure up that sense of breathing. There's a number of piano players, jazz and classical, who of course are fantastic at that. You could say the same about some drummers and vibes players. We all have the same mandate, in a way: we try to communicate the kinds of phrases that would be believable if somebody were singing them."

Some people resist jazz guitar playing, Metheny said, because guitar players don't convey that sense of breath. "Saxophonists have a very wide dynamic range. They're dealing with a ratio of about *that.*" He spread his hands to indicate a foot. "With guitar we have a ratio of about this"—he spread his thumb and index finger to indicate about four inches—"in terms of what we can do with our touch."

Some pianists would play this music with a more smoothed-out phrasing, I said, more legato than Gould. Metheny replied that what he loves about Gould's phrasing is that he makes music become almost physical, palpitating. Long ago, the vibraphonist Gary Burton had insisted that Metheny listen to more Gould for precisely this reason.

"No two notes there are ever the same volume. He's constantly doing this"—he poked and prodded the air. "It's like, it's so *alive*. How many shades of dynamics can you play with? With the guitar, you really have to model in your mind this wider thing; you're trying to create the illusion of a bigger dynamic range.

"The guy who defined that, on guitar," he said, on a roll now, "was Jim Hall, who opened up five or six degrees of dynamics on both sides by picking softer. He could then make certain things jump out a little bit more. Certainly the three of us who often get grouped together—me, John Scofield, and Bill Frisell—all of us have adopted that general touch on the instrument." But, he said, Hall remains the standard. "In jazz, I don't know that we've ever had any other nonwind instrument player who has as much detailed, deep control over dynamics, who really has both extremes. Because"—at least when it comes to electric guitar—"you can play really, really loud, but he also has one of the most fantastic pianissimos of all time."

Two hours into our marathon of listening and talking, Metheny seemed as fresh as when he came in. Preferring to continue without a break, he ate a snack and kept going. Near the end, in the early evening, we got around to his favorite guitar solo of all time: Wes Montgomery's chorus and a half on "If You Could See Me Now," from *Smokin' at the Half Note*, recorded in 1965 by the Wynton Kelly Trio with Wes Montgomery.

As a young musician, Metheny did everything he could to sound like Montgomery, including playing without a pick and improvising parallel lines an octave apart. "But when I was fourteen or fifteen," he said, "I realized that what I was doing was really disrespectful, because that wasn't me, that was him. I grew up in Lee's Summit, Missouri. I didn't grow up in New York City. I'm white; I'm not black. I'm from a little town where you couldn't help but hear country music, and I loved it. I always wanted to address those things with certain notes, qualities of chords, kinds of voice-leading." He cued up the solo. We listened once, then listened again while he talked.

"This is such an incredibly strong melodic opening," he said, during the first four bars of the solo, before Montgomery moves into triplet patterns in bars five through eight. "And also, that first phrase is pretty full, like a full speaking voice, but then"—at bars three and four—"he's really soft here. It's almost like Glenn Gould; every note's a different volume."

In the second chorus, the band starts to swing harder, and Montgomery plays powerful, earthy phrases in the second A section. "Then there's the blues factor in all of this, too, which he just tucks in there." Toward the end of each section, Montgomery forecasts the beginning of the next part, building some tension; each time Metheny heard this, he looked ecstatic. "He's starting a new thing, setting it up. And now, look at this"—during the second chorus—"just quarter notes. He gets two or three levels above the time, and then gets right back in the pocket."

"It's really hard to play a short solo," Metheny said, when the track was finished. "Like an eight-bar solo. Every single thing about it has to count. And that's like Bach, almost."

Metheny's pronouncement in the *Times* that B-flat minor was "the saddest of all keys" quickly appeared on several blogs about music, as a Deep Thought. Neither the bloggers nor I had realized that Metheny was quoting from *This Is Spinal Tap.* He was going so fast that the reference went right past me.

In the movie, Marty DiBergi, the documentary filmmaker (played by Rob Reiner), is listening to Nigel Tufnel, Spinal Tap's guitarist-singer-songwriter (played by Christopher Guest), practice a melancholy piece on the piano. "It's very pretty," says DiBergi.

"Yeah, I like it," Tufnel says. "I've been fooling around with it for a few months now. It's very delicate."

"It's a bit of a departure from the kind of thing you normally play."

"It's part of a trilogy, really, a musical trilogy that I'm doing in D minor, which I always find is really the saddest of all keys. Really. I don't know why, but it makes people weep instantly."

When I e-mailed Metheny about this later, he was glad to learn that I had only been slow on the uptake. He had worried that my printing his quote as spoken, without proper annotation, was an act of mock-serious irony, to counteract his act of mock-serious irony, which would have been building on the original mock-serious irony in the film. "I think that is one too many," he wrote, "and may well be illegal in some states." The overarching irony, he pointed out, is that E-flat minor is, in fact, truly the saddest of all keys.

Set List

Sonny Rollins and Coleman Hawkins (with Paul Bley), "All the Things You Are," from *Sonny Meets Hawk!* (RCA/BMG), recorded 1963.
Miles Davis, "Seven Steps to Heaven," from *The Complete Concert 1964: My Funny Valentine and Four & More* (Sony Legacy), recorded 1964.

J. S. Bach, Fugue no. 22 in B-flat Minor, from *The Well-Tempered Clavier,* Book 1, Glenn Gould, piano (Sony Classical), recorded 1965.

Antonio Carlos Jobim, "Passarim," from *Passarim* (Verve), recorded 1987.

Wynton Kelly Trio with Wes Montgomery, "If You Could See Me Now," from *Smokin' at the Half Note* (Verve), recorded 1965.

3

Jazz Means Freedom

Sonny Rollins

His face and neatly trimmed white beard shaded by a Filson hunting cap, Sonny Rollins had just arrived from a visit to the dentist. The dentist is more or less his only reason to make the two-and-a-half-hour trip to New York City anymore, unless he's giving an infrequent concert.

The tenor saxophonist—who is, according to semiregular consensus from the most authoritative sources, the greatest living improviser in jazz—lives on a farm in Germantown, in Columbia County, New York, a property he bought in 1972 with his wife, Lucille. They had once also kept an apartment on Greenwich Street, in lower Manhattan's TriBeCa neighborhood, but his wife had come to enjoy the city less and less, especially after the destruction of the World Trade Center towers, six blocks away. (Rollins had been in the thirty-ninth-floor apartment during the attacks.) Lucille, who also acted as Rollins's manager and record producer, died in November 2004—a little less than a year before I met with him in 2005—of complications from a stroke. He was going through a period of transition.

Rollins seems to have genuine humility, the private kind. In the high-ceilinged lobby of the old New York Times building on Forty-third Street, a staff photographer—who didn't know him personally but had taken his picture before—greeted him in that reverent-but-familiar register that a long-standing fan can use with a great jazz musician. Rollins doesn't need a street retinue as, say, Keith Richards might. But he inspires much the same kind of devotion. Admiringly, the man raised his hand to Rollins's shoulder. Rollins shrank.

As we rode the elevator, I asked him how his concert had gone at that summer's Montreal Jazz Festival, the week previous. "Well, I don't know," he answered in his froggy voice. "I look at all that from the inside, so you'd probably have to ask someone else." He wore a wine-colored ascot, and though he kept his dark blue rain-coat on indoors throughout the morning, he seemed relaxed. When he felt self-conscious, he talked about it.

For a musician who has lived under a nearly unshoulderable load of praise, Rollins's tendency toward self-criticism appears paralyzing: if he can't trust others, and he can't trust himself, then what? But on the subject of music other than his own, his responses were undogmatic, free. And fairly fresh. He said, regretfully, that for twenty years he had not really listened much to music, so as to protect himself from too much information.

He had just released a live album, *Without a Song*, a recording of a Boston concert made three days after the September 11 attacks. It was the first in a possible series of live Sonny Rollins recordings to be released to the general market. Carl Smith, a retired lawyer from

Maine who also collects jazz recordings, had located (and in a few cases, including the Boston concert, surreptitiously recorded) more than 350 Rollins performances, going back to a three-minute Rollins solo on alto saxophone from 1948. Were all of these performances to be made available, they would be taken very seriously in the jazz world, because Rollins's studio records of the last thirty years—some would say forty—have scarcely indicated the extent of his talent.

A powerful, grand-scale improviser, Rollins often needs half an hour or more to say what he wants on the horn and get his momentum. Once, he recalled, he played a two-and-a-half-hour solo in a club, completely forgetting the house policy of clearing the audience for a second set. (He imagines a vocational link between himself and the whirling dervishes of Istanbul.) He has also been a paragon of structure as he improvises. Almost every modern jazz musician is fascinated by Sonny Rollins.

Rollins and Smith were able to reach a place of mutual trust, and in 2007 Rollins was persuaded to release tapes of his 1957 concert at Carnegie Hall, on his own label, Doxy. But, even after he went public with his decision about the Carnegie tapes, he still had not listened to them. Not long after, he scrapped the plan.

He has an aversion to hearing himself play. However, to make good on an agreement with his former record company, Milestone, he had to force himself to listen closely to the tape of his September 14, 2001, concert, a process that he described as "like Abu Ghraib."

"It's possible for me to hear something I did and say, 'yeah, I like that,'" Rollins admitted. "Although it would probably never be a whole thing. Maybe a section of something, or a solo."

* * *

Rollins was born in 1930 of parents who had come to New York City from the Virgin Islands. He grew up in Harlem—first in the lowlands around 135th Street and Lenox Avenue, and then, starting at nine, in the Sugar Hill neighborhood, a locus at the time for the city's jazz musicians. He attended Benjamin Franklin High School in what was then an Italian section of East Harlem, and lived through an early New York experiment in busing black students to white neighborhoods; he remembers people throwing objects at the bus windows. It was such a high-profile case of school integration that Frank Sinatra and Nat King Cole gave concerts to the students in the school auditorium to promote race relations.

Thinking of his childhood, Rollins wanted to hear Fats Waller's 1934 recording of "I'm Going to Sit Right Down and Write Myself a Letter." (It was the top of a list of choices that he had sent me with almost automatic efficiency, ten weeks in advance.) From the beginning of the song Rollins looked as if he had just stepped into a warm bath. A clarinetist began playing counterpoint improvisations against Waller's piano and voice.

"Who's the clarinet player?" Rollins asked, coming out of his reverie.

It was Rudy Powell. "Isn't that something?" he said. "I went to school with Rudy Powell's son." Rollins and the senior Rudy Powell didn't know each other, although they stood about three feet apart in Art Kane's famous "Great Day in Harlem" photograph from 1958.

"I remember hearing that song around the house, and on the radio and everything," Rollins said when it finished. "It's one of my earliest memories of jazz. I believe in things like reincarnation, and it struck a chord someplace in my back lives or something."

It's very restful, I said, as we listened to the song again. It's not the other Fats Waller, the boisterous one. There's a little rude joke in the words, but he plays it subtle.

"Yeah," Rollins agreed. "He could be raucous, but this is very, very much—mmm." (Waller was singing: "I'm gonna write words oh so sweet/they're gonna knock me off my feet/a lot of kisses on the bottom/I'll be glad I got 'em.")

"*Yeah*," Rollins said, still impressed by Powell, after we listened again. "But the thing I want to stress," he said, "is that this is evocative of the whole Harlem scene. Where I was born, when I was born. And his playing, that stride piano style which of course comes from other people. It's overwhelming to me, really. When I hear him, to me it just says the whole thing. It encapsulates jazz, the spirit of jazz. In a very overall way."

We moved on to Coleman Hawkins. If Waller represents Rollins's childhood, Hawkins represents his maturation. (An infatuation with Louis Jordan came in between.) Around the time Rollins got keenly interested in the saxophone, as a teenager in the mid-1940s, Hawkins was especially hot. In late 1943, the year-long ban imposed by the American Federation of Musicians, preventing commercial recordings, had just been lifted, and Hawkins, nearing forty and very competitive, was making up for lost time, collaborating with the younger beboppers.

"The Man I Love," from December 1943, is one of the greatest performances in jazz, though overshadowed by Hawkins's much more famous recording of "Body and Soul." It was released on a twelve-inch 78 RPM record—a detail Rollins remembered—because Hawkins had too much to say and started a second chorus. It ended at 5:05, too long for the normal ten-inch format.

This part of Hawkins, his flow of ideas, has special resonance for Rollins. By 1957 or so, Rollins was using jazz to deliver a more accurate reflection of how his mind worked; the music wasn't just tightly framed, mediated entertainment, but a record of everything he was thinking in a certain place at a certain hour, with all the surging ahead and backtracking and repeating that are natural pathways in everyday consciousness. He—along with John Coltrane, around the same time—changed the way jazz audiences listened; suddenly it was more possible to understand jazz from the musicians' perspective.

We listened to Hawkins's two voluminous choruses, ambitious from the very opening phrase: an E-natural chord jostling against an E-flat. "You know, he's doing a lot of stuff in there, man," said Rollins, at the end. "Very far-reaching, too. Coleman was a guy that played chord changes in an up-and-down manner. He sort of played every change, let me put it that way. He had a phrase for every change that went by. So in that solo he was not only playing the changes, he was also playing the passing chords, which is another thing he was ahead of his time on. And still, he was getting the jazz intensity moving, so he was building and building and building . . . Yeah"—he nodded—"it's a work of art."

When did he get around to Coleman Hawkins? "Well, 'Body and Soul' was ubiquitous in Harlem, on jukeboxes. They could have turned me on to him. But since I moved up on the hill, where so many of these guys lived, I even had a chance to see him driving around. He had an impressive Cadillac. He dressed well. And, you know, there were certain other people that acted more on the entertainment side. There was even a time in my life when I had a brief feeling about Louis Armstrong, that he was too minstrel-y and too smiley. That didn't last long. I was a young person at the time. But what impressed me about Coleman was that he carried himself with great dignity."

A lot of Rollins's heroes lived in his neighborhood: Denzil Best, the drummer who played with Hawkins and composed the bebop standard "Move"; Eddie Lockjaw Davis, the saxophonist; the god Hawkins himself. The tricky part was getting their ear, to ask them questions about their playing, or just to be in their presence. "There was a great photographer named James J. Kriegsman," he remembered, who used to make these pictures of musicians, and he made a beautiful picture of Coleman. So I had my eight-by-ten, and I knew where he lived, up on 153rd Street, and one day I knew when he was coming home. He signed my autograph. That was one of the first times I was that close to him. I was thirteen or fourteen.

"I used to go down to see him on Fifty-second Street," he continued. "We had to put on eyebrow pencil to make it look like we had real mustaches, to look older. I was still strictly amateur; I wasn't that good yet to play with those guys.

"I was a real pest, as a young guy," he decided. "When I found out we lived near Denzil Best, and that my mother knew a woman who knew him, I used to go by and ring his bell. One time, I knew the guy was there, so I just kept ringing and ringing. Finally, he opened it. He was half-sleepy. So I asked him some questions about playing with Coleman Hawkins. He was just"—he growled—"'*Get this kid out of here.*'"

About twenty years later, in 1963, Rollins made a record with Hawkins, one of the most psychologically fraught records in jazz. It says something about Rollins's self-possession, and the quality of his respect for his hero, that he didn't just fold and defer completely to Hawkins. In fact, he did the opposite, playing *around* him.

"We had played together at Newport, and that sort of broke the ice. But when we made the record, I was particularly *trying* to sound different. I felt I had heard a lot of people play with Coleman, a lot of tenor players. I heard this thing with him and Ben Webster; they did some beautiful stuff. And one with Webster and Georgie Auld, three saxophonists. Anyway, I had a very contemporary band: I had Paul Bley; I had Henry Grimes. We considered ourselves to be breaking the envelope and doing very contemporary things," he explained. "I didn't want to change that with Coleman. I wanted him to relate to what we were doing, which was completely legitimate. A lot of younger guys—Miles Davis, Monk—had come up playing with Coleman. It was nothing he couldn't handle."

Rollins had asked to hear Billie Holiday singing "Lover Man." I had brought it, but it wasn't what he was looking for. I had a live version of the song, from a television show in 1955; Rollins wanted the one in his head, the studio version from 1944, her last hit. "Her voice was a little more worn on that one," he said, after hearing the 1955 track. "But Billie Holiday worn is still great to me. It's just that on that first 'Lover Man' her voice had a different quality— clearer, maybe."

She did move, over time, toward sounding as if she were very conscious of her own stylization, I said. Earlier there had been more of a sense that it was just coming out of her.

"I've experienced this myself," Rollins replied. "People expect you to play exactly like you made a record. In my case, I didn't have to worry, because I never play anything the same anyway. But in Billie's case, I could see where she was trying to sing like the record. I can see how, for her, it could have been a problem. Do you understand what I mean?" he asked, working to finesse what seemed like a simple point. "She was trying to do what she did on the record more precisely than other people might."

I guessed that he was in there with her for the whole thing— even the recordings from the end of her career when her voice was much diminished, the albums like *Lady in Satin*, which some find almost morbid.

"Oh, yeah," he said, with certainty. "I have to be. At the very end, I was definitely with her, because then I knew what was going on in her life. If anything, I felt so much empathy that I didn't look at it so much as a musical thing; I looked at it more as a life thing.

"I always loved Billie Holiday," he declared. "I had a crush on her as a younger person. She was really a beautiful woman, and I was around her a couple of times. And finally I got to play"—he corrected himself—"well, I never played with Billie Holiday. But I played at a place where I played opposite her," meaning that his own band appeared on the same multiple bill. "We were working at this place out in New Jersey—it might have been the Cherry Hill Club, in Cherry Hill—and we were staying at the Walt Whitman Hotel, in Camden. So we had to drive to the club every day, and I got to know a lovely person.

"Oh, boy." He sighed. "It was sad. Because of all her drug problems, everybody knew about all the stuff she was going through. She was actually being abused by some of these club owners and agents. Listening to these guys hollering at her about being on time—it really upset me."

Rollins didn't notice drug dealers closing in around her at that time. (I wasn't thinking about it when we talked, but at the time he knew Holiday, Rollins might have been rigorously avoiding even looking at a drug dealer. He had had a heroin habit himself, which he finally kicked in 1955 at the federal narcotics hospital in Lexington, Kentucky.) "I remember, then, that she was moving up to one of those streets off of Central Park West. I took her home one time, and I didn't see any drug people. But to me she was a sweet, vulnerable woman. She was gentle. She would cuss with everybody, but inside she was soft as a kitten."

Inevitably, Charlie Parker had been on Rollins's list. But the piece—"Another Hair Do," from 1947—was an unusual choice. It is a twelve-bar blues. At the beginning, Parker and a very young Miles Davis play a repeated line for the first four bars. But then Parker cuts loose, improvising by himself at double-speed for five bars, before the written part resumes and the theme ends.

"Another Hair Do" is nothing canonical in jazz history, but for Rollins it was. "The thing about this song was that the form of it was revolutionary even for bop," he said.

He started from the top. "First of all, this guy's rhythmic thing was definitely on another planet. You don't find people doing that, the way he was doubling up the tempo there. There was a lot of free improvisation in the melody there." (By *melody,* Rollins meant the opening twelve-bar theme section.)

When Parker comes back to play the theme again, I said, he's not going to play that fast bit the same way. "No," Rollins said. "It's an open space. See, Miles is trying to do a little bit of it too"— improvising in double time over the steady pulse—"but he can't quite do it yet. But, you know, Miles was a genius. He was playing with Charlie Parker and not able to do some of the technical stuff, but yet making it sound like he's in the same ballpark."

He whistled and laughed. "It's not just the computer saying four notes against two notes. It's what Charlie Parker's doing within that thing. It's music that can't be written down. You have to *feel* that to make it come out. But what Charlie Parker accomplished was, he made an open-ended song which was not open-ended. It *wasn't* like playing anything you want. But within that there was so much freedom to play what you wanted to play. And still he made it to sound like a regular blues song."

Rollins himself wrote some open-ended pieces, I said. Like "The Bridge," or even "Oleo." The melody of "Oleo" follows the chord changes of "I Got Rhythm," but in the B section there's no written melody; it's a blank canvas every time it's played.

"Well, I probably got them from my idol there," he responded. "There's a certain freedom within his playing which we have to strive for. People playing jazz have to try to understand where he was coming from, what that was, and emulate it and absorb it. This is what jazz is: jazz means freedom. I don't think you always have to play in time. But there's two different ways of playing. There's a way of playing where you can play with no time. Or you can have a fixed time and play against it. That's what I feel is *heaven*, being able to be that free, spiritual, musical. I would say that's an ideal which is underappreciated."

Here he seemed to sense that he was getting into rough waters. "I mean playing free without any kind of time strictures—there's nothing wrong with that either. But I think that—gee, I don't know—I'm probably going to be dissing myself to the new guys coming up somewhere, but a lot of our audiences still relate to time. I'm still in the era of time being an important component of jazz. So kill me."

* * *

Finally we got around to Lester Young. "Afternoon of a Basie-Ite" was recorded in 1943—strangely enough, five days after Coleman Hawkins's "The Man I Love" session—with a quartet including Johnny Guarnieri on piano, Slam Stewart on bass, and Sid Catlett on drums. It is almost lotus-eater music, light and gorgeous, geared toward dancing. "Boy, I'm telling you," said Rollins, smiling. "That's the Savoy ballroom there.

"It sounds very free and easy," Rollins went on to say. "But we know it's not, because what he's saying is deep as the ocean. There was a beginning and an end. He was storytelling all the way through. So when I first heard that, I mean, this cat was *talking*."

When you talk about improvised storytelling, I asked him, what are you really talking about?

He belly-laughed. "Well, I guess it's making sense. It's like talking gibberish and making sense. That's on the very basic level. Then beyond that, of course, it's a beautiful story. It's uplifting. It's emotional."

He wanted to illustrate it further with an observation a writer once made about his playing, but then he stopped himself. "I don't want this to sound self-aggrandizing. In my later years I've become very self-effacing. I don't mean this to seem like I'm talking about great people. You must indulge me in that. I have decided that I know what greatness is, and I don't want to put myself in that category."

Understood. "Anyway," he continued, "somebody wrote that what I was doing in a certain song was asking a question and then answering the question. I think he was talking about harmonic resolutions. So that would be sort of what I think telling a story might be: resolving a thought."

I asked if there were any of his own recorded performances he felt comfortable with, that didn't pain him with thoughts of how it could have been better. "It's hard to say, because I haven't listened to any of my stuff in a long time. Unless it's on the radio, and I can't leave the room. But I seem to like 'Sonnymoon for Two,' with Elvin Jones and Wilbur Ware." (It can be found on Rollins's album *A Night at the Village Vanguard*, from 1957.) "That's not my optimum, but I like certain things I did on that."

I asked if the increasing self-effacement he spoke about had any musical implications. Does it come out in his work?

Rollins looked embarrassed and tickled by the idea. He started smiling and looking at the corners of the room, as if wondering whether there was an escape hatch. "Wow. Well, I hope that it's going to be expressed in my work. But I don't know how. These things come out." His hands flew up to his face, and he twisted the white strands of beard around his mouth, grinning.

Set List

Fats Waller, "I'm Going to Sit Right Down and Write Myself a Letter," from *The Very Best of Fats Waller* (RCA/BMG), recorded 1934.

Coleman Hawkins, "The Man I Love," from *Coleman Hawkins, 1943–1944* (Classics), recorded 1943.

Billie Holiday, "Lover Man," from *Billie Holiday: Rare Live Recordings 1934–1959* (ESP-Disk), recorded 1955.

Charlie Parker, "Another Hair Do," from *The Complete Savoy and Dial Studio Recordings, 1944–1948* (Savoy Jazz), recorded 1947.

Lester Young, "Afternoon of a Basie-Ite," *The Complete Lester Young on Keynote* (Polygram), recorded 1943.

4

As Good as You Think

Andrew Hill

In the precocious early days of his nightclub work, the jazz pianist Andrew Hill traveled from Chicago to Detroit to play with Charlie Parker. It was a gig with a pickup band; Parker had called them to back him up for a job at the Greystone Ballroom, one of Detroit's dance palaces. From that first encounter with Parker, Hill ended up with more than a line on his résumé.

Hill's past has been notoriously hard to put together, and his memory has been spotty about when this happened; when pressed, he would say 1948, or sometimes 1952. But Parker's movements are roughly trackable, and there are eyewitnesses: the pianist Barry Harris, among others, can testify to being there that night. Harris and some jazz historians are in agreement that it was probably April 1954. Calculating by the birth date that Andrew Hill preferred to use before his death in April 2007, he would then have been sixteen.

In any case, he and Parker were talking about music, and Hill said that Parker told him this: "I look at melody as rhythm." A stray comment led to a long preoccupation.

As a jazz composer, Hill was as original as they come. From the start he had only a modest following. He arrived in New York City in 1960, to join Roland Kirk's group. When he started making his own records for Blue Note a few years later, he didn't make a great public splash, as Ornette Coleman had in 1959, or even keep a working band to establish a presence in the clubs. Instead, he played the college circuit, taught, and applied for arts grants. At one point, in a 1966 interview in *Down Beat*, he encouraged each of his listeners to send him a dollar.

Slight and kindly, with soft eyes and old-world manners, Hill delivered his ideas in bursts of information, often ending in a question. He had a stutter—it was in his style of playing piano as well—and the way he phrased stories about his life, or his responses to music, left them open to interpretation.

"Am I confusing you?" he asked during our afternoon listening to music and talking about what he heard in it. "Is the truth confusing?"

For the last seven years of his life, Hill lived in a well-kept Victorian brownstone in Jersey City, New Jersey, with elegant old furniture in a front living room and a baby grand piano in the back; when I was there, a book of sheet music for Bach's preludes and fugues lay open on it. As I moved around the room, he saw my eyes go to the piano, and he feigned alarm when I wrote down the page on display. "Oh, no," he said. "Don't tell the world that I can read." The joke, it seemed to me, was about how few incontrovertible truths the world knew about him.

He and his wife, Joanne Robinson Hill, the director of education at the Joyce Theater for dance in New York, settled there after his return from a long sojourn on the West Coast. His first wife,

Laverne, died in California in 1989; after that, until 1996, he taught at Portland State University in Oregon, where he met Joanne.

Hill had been enduring his fight against lung cancer when I checked in with him in 2006. He looked tired but peaceful. ("You're normally only as good as you think, anyway," he said, coughing. "That's all there is.") We sat in his front room. Hearing some of the music he knows best filled him with enthusiasm—for his audiences, among other things. His talk kept coming around to his gratitude that people have cared about his work for so long.

Hill was born in Chicago in 1931—not Port-au-Prince, Haiti, as his early biographies read, and not in 1937, as he often stated. He grew up on Chicago's South Side. He was reluctant to say what his parents did—or perhaps did not quite fully know himself—except that they were "part of the struggling environment for their generation," and that they did not block his path as a musician. From age three to seven, he said, he remained in a state that he describes as semiautistic; he didn't respond adequately in social situations. "I wasn't ready to accept my socioeconomic position," he explained. "By not recognizing it, I could escape it."

He evolved, he said, by playing music. He started on a child's accordion, graduating to a proper button accordion at age seven, and taught himself piano at ten from the player piano in his home. He balanced his high-school work with extra classes for gifted students at the University of Chicago's lab school and played accordion on the street for extra money; he positioned himself on a corner of the South Side, at Forty-seventh Street and South Parkway, near the Regal Theater and the Savoy Ballroom.

It has always been hard to place Hill within jazz's spectrum. He started playing jazz when bebop was a popular music, and played it in the company of the best. But when he moved to New York in 1960, he stood on the periphery of a self-conscious vanguard that was exploding jazz's basic elements and functions, pushing it toward abstraction and social consciousness. He wrote a great deal of dense, nettling music, which often turned out—curiously, with repeated exposure—to be songlike and pleasurable. It is difficult to play, and he consistently hired, at each point in his career, the most authoritative musicians in jazz to help him bring it to life: Lee Morgan, Ron Carter, Roy Haynes, Bobby Hutcherson, Greg Osby. This continued with his final quintet, one of his best. That band included Charles Tolliver on trumpet, who played with Hill in the late 1960s, though the rest of the players—the saxophonist and clarinetist Greg Tardy, the bassist John Hebert, and the drummer Eric McPherson—were all a generation younger. Throughout, Hill was impossible to identify as either inside or outside the jazz mainstream. But whereas this worked against him for at least thirty years, by the end history was on his side. Jazz musicians have been increasingly bending the loose ends of history toward each other, making sense of the fractures between tradition and innovation or coming to understand that those fractures may be illusory.

In 2005, after being signed by Blue Note for the third time in forty-two years, Hill made a superb album, *Time Lines*. It was his last. As usual, it was full of Charlie Parker's inadvertent lesson, melody-as-rhythm. (Even the title seemed to play on the idea: *time* as in rhythm, *lines* as in melody.) Commanding rhythms keep rising out of the stop-start melodic phrases; with pecking repetitions, Hill elongates parts of them at will. Like Thelonious Monk, he made his music sound as if its theme sections are improvised and the improvised sections are composed. And like Monk's, his music is a balanced equation, with melody embedded in harmony and overlapping rhythms swimming in agreement. It has a mysteriously powerful internal integrity.

His work is dense and knotty and difficult to play, but much of it is beautiful, aerated with song. Sometimes it reduces into absolute parts—two bars in one meter, four bars in another. (He liked switching between meters, and he liked unusual ones.) And sometimes it doesn't; instead, there's an undefined, shifting-sands feeling.

Alfred Lion, one of the founders of Blue Note, was beguiled by Hill in the early 1960s. As he had done with two other pianists, Monk and Herbie Nichols, he encouraged Hill to record as many of his compositions as possible for his label, as quickly as he could. So Hill made five records in the first eight months after signing with Blue Note in 1963. Among these are *Smokestack*, *Point of Departure*, and *Black Fire*, three of the great records of the era. In all, from 1963 to 1970, Hill recorded nineteen albums for Blue Note, too much for the market to bear; only eight were released at the time. (Two more were released in his second period with the label, from 1989 to 1990.)

In the last five years of Hill's life, he teamed up with another champion of his work: Michael Cuscuna, the founder of Mosaic, the CD reissue company, and the producer of *Time Lines*. Starting in 2002, Cuscuna reissued all the music Hill made for Blue Note, even the sessions that were never before released.

All in all, Hill had won.

His first choice of music to listen to during my visit was Charlie Parker's most famous blues, "Now's the Time," from 1945. He called it "the perfect record."

Hill understood Parker's comment about melody as rhythm as a refutation of the "Eurocentric" music education he had grown up with—where melody is paramount, harmony accompanies it, and rhythm is the last part to worry about. "It opened my mind up to many possibilities," he said. "If everything is rhythm, then you just have these rhythms on top of each other. But they're not polyrhythms or pyramids of rhythm; they're crossing rhythms."

"Now's the Time" is driven by a short, syncopated melody with a strong rhythm, putting down a bounce in almost every beat. "In that period, one could pretend that one could hear," Hill said. "You didn't have to read it to understand it. It was all around you. And I guess because it had a blues sensibility, it was inclusive of more people."

I said that given his interest in the idea of melody as rhythm, I thought he would have suggested a bebop tune with a more complicatedly rhythmic line, like Miles Davis's "Donna Lee." "There was something lovely about hearing those fast tempos," he replied, "like 'Donna Lee' or '52nd Street Theme.' But with the blues, one doesn't have to be a space scientist to get the harmony. 'Donna Lee' has more changes—bringing you in more than letting you out."

We listened to Fats Navarro and Gil Fuller's "Webb City," from 1946; Bud Powell, who cowrote the tune, is the pianist on the record, and his solo is a bebop masterpiece, delivered in curling streams of single notes. "This is almost the same area," he said. "But it's not entrapped harmonically; it's not so demanding as 'Donna Lee,'" he decided. "Another good example of melody as rhythm."

The song finished. "'Now's the Time' had that call-and-response blues that brought me in," he remembered. "And then there were the parts between the drums and the saxophones. Through the years, I've always said to myself that when the drums and the saxophone play together, that's a dance, which is an aspect of melody as rhythm. Mm?"

He paused to think. "But 'Webb City,' the way Bud Powell was playing," he continued, "that was the next step."

Did he go through a period, like many of his contemporaries, of wanting to play like Bud Powell, who established the common bebop language for the piano the way Parker had done for saxophone?

"In general," he answered evenly, with a rising tone at the end, "I was very analytical about the ways you can learn?"

Next on his list was "Blue Rondo à la Turk," from Dave Brubeck's fluke-hit 1959 album, *Time Out*. The song is famous for its meter shifts: it flicks between a fast 9/8 and an easy, midtempo 4/4 swing, though it doesn't try to make them flow into each other.

"I keep hearing the different rhythm-melodies," Hill said as the song played. "The rhythm-melody that the drummer plays, for example. But this also represents when people weren't as comfortable playing rhythms like that"—he meant the 9/8—"all the way through numbers, as they are now."

With pieces like this, Brubeck made jazz seem sensible for many who came to it cold; it's a playful piece of music and very schematic. He phrased almost right on the beat and kept swing roped off in the song's 4/4 section. When Hill played, on the other hand, he moved around the beat, never playing on it, and not consistently behind it or ahead of it, either.

"Yes, peaceful coexistence," Hill said when I brought up his relation to the beat. "It's always been like that."

The next piece was "As Long as You're Living," by the Max Roach Plus Four group. Also recorded in 1959, it is a blues in 5/4 time, like Brubeck's "Take Five." (Playing jazz in five was new then. Roach was said to be irritated at Mercury, his label, for withholding the release of "As Long as You're Living" until after "Take Five" became a hit.)

It's a little masterpiece, sleek and grooving, with all the solemn bravado of Roach's music in that period. And the Roach band demonstrates that a five-beat rhythm can be swung as fluidly as the usual 4/4. "It shows the progression of how people become more comfortable with this rhythm," Hill said. "With 'Blue Rondo à la Turk,' one is disappointed that they don't continue the rhythm through the number. But here they do, and they have it down like a four."

For the last piece of the afternoon, Hill got away from time signatures and back to his youth. He picked a solo piano piece by Earl Hines, the standard "Wrap Your Troubles in Dreams," recorded in 1974 at a private party in California.

"He was a very nice man," Hill said of Hines. "When I met him, I was eight or nine. He played at this club, the Grand Terrace Ballroom, and he had a penthouse in the hotel where the lounge was on the bottom floor. I was his paperboy," Hill recalled with a high-pitched laugh. "The *Chicago Tribune*."

Hines thinks fast and broadly through the performance of "Wrap Your Troubles in Dreams." He keeps inserting new rhythms and rubato sections; the performance becomes free-associative. It has sweeping two-handed runs in it, the kind of thing Art Tatum liked to do, and with them he rewrites the song in real time.

This was an example, Hill explained, of what jazz virtuosos like Hines called concertizing—making concert-hall fantasias of tunes, often by themselves in nightclubs. "You know," he said,

"Benny Goodman took his band to Carnegie Hall. But black musicians at the time started consciously elaborating on melodies in a different way. They'd take it over the bar lines, or do whatever."

So it's not so much that Hines is implying "this is the straight part," and "this is where I'm stretching it," and "now I go back to the straight part," I said. It's all mixed together, all the way through.

"What impressed me about him the most was that he enjoyed himself," Hill responded. "He was successful, and the people were with him. When a person has a message for the people, he's usually heard and well taken care of. The rest is what they think of themselves. You know, like Charlie Parker—people loved him. They treated him so much better than he treated himself. I mean, it's such a big honor to have people support you. That's quite a bit."

Set List

Charlie Parker, "Now's the Time," from *The Genius of Charlie Parker* (Savoy Jazz), recorded 1945.

Fats Navarro/Gil Fuller's Modernists, "Webb City," from *Goin' to Minton's* (Savoy Jazz), recorded 1946.

Dave Brubeck, "Blue Rondo à la Turk," from *Time Out* (Sony Legacy), recorded 1959.

Max Roach Plus Four, "As Long as You're Living," from *The Complete Mercury Max Roach Plus Four Sessions* (Mosaic), recorded 1959.

Earl Hines, "Wrap Your Troubles in Dreams (and Dream Your Troubles Away)," from *Solo Piano* (LaserLight), recorded 1974.

5

I Know Who You Are

Ornette Coleman

The alto saxophonist and composer Ornette Coleman, like Sonny Rollins one of the last truly imposing figures in jazz from a generation full of them, seldom talks about other people's music. But then people, especially journalists, generally want to ask him about his own, and so that becomes the subject he addresses. Or half-addresses; what he's really focused on is a set of interrelated questions about music, religion, and ontology. At times he can seem purposefully confusing or sentimental. Other times he comes across as one of the world's killer aphorists. Depending on the issue, he flickers back and forth between belief and skepticism.

On the telephone, a few days before we met, I asked him what he would like to listen to. "Anything you want," he said, in his fluty southern voice. "There is no bad music, only bad performances." He finally offered a few suggestions. The music he likes is simply defined: anything that can't be summed up in a common term; any music that is not created as part of a style. "The state of surviving in music is more like 'what music are you playing,'" he said. "But music isn't a style; it's an idea. The idea of music, without it being a style—I don't hear that much anymore."

Then he went up a level. "I would like to have the same concept of ideas as how people believe in God," he said. "To me, an idea doesn't have any master."

To a certain way of thinking, Coleman solved it all a long time ago. The records he made for Atlantic, with his various quartets from 1959 to 1961, are unreasonably beautiful. His music bears a tight sense of knowing itself, of natural form. Born in 1930 and raised in Fort Worth, Texas, he attained some skill at playing rhythm and blues in bars during the late 1940s and early '50s, like any other decent saxophonist. He arrived in New York (via Los Angeles) with an original, logical sense of melody and an idea of playing with no preconceived chord changes.

His New York debut inspired a character in Thomas Pynchon's *V* named McClintic Sphere, and established an unshakable reputation in serious-art circles as a kind of outsider genius. Following the initial onslaught came a short period with a trio. He then disappeared from recording in 1963 and 1964, before emerging with another trio again, followed by a fantastic quartet, from 1968 to 1972, with the tenor saxophonist Dewey Redman. Then came a period of funk-through-the-looking glass with his electric band, Prime Time.

Even in his seventies, Coleman continued to move. In recent years, before I met with him in 2006, he had been working with a new band including two bassists, Greg Cohen and Tony Falanga, and his son, Denardo Coleman, who plays his own version of rhythm—jury-rigged, rushing, often quite loud. Denardo's drumming would probably be unthinkable in any other jazz group, and perhaps this is why his father has preferred it for so long. The quartet was playing about twenty-five concerts a year, making music that, despite the change in instrumentation, held a certain distant similarity to what he had been doing when he was thirty.

Coleman has a kind of high-end generosity; he claimed that he wouldn't think twice about letting me go home with a piece of music he had just written, no questions asked, because he would be interested in what I might make of it. But there was some pessimism in his talk, too. He insisted that no review or article had ever helped his career. (This is hard to understand, as since the late 1970s he has received some of the most elaborate, down-on-hands-and-knees, explanations-of-method jobs in the history of jazz criticism.) He explained that most of the history of humanity had been wasted on building increasingly complicated class structures. "Life is already complete," he said. "You can't learn what life is. And the only way you die is if something kills you. So if life and death are already understood, what are we doing?"

On *Sound Grammar*, the live album he released in 2006 on his new record label of the same name, lines travel together and pull apart, following the curve of his melodies, tangling and playing in a unison that allows for discrepancies between individual sound and intonation and, sometimes, key. Like most of his other records, it sold very little and received stupendous reviews. Unlike any of his other records, it won him a Pulitzer Prize.

Unison is one of his favorite words; he puts an almost mystical significance on it, and he uses it in many different ways. "Being a human, you're required to be in unison: upright," he said.

Coleman draws you into the chicken-and-egg riddles that he asks himself. These questions can become the dark side of Bible class. Many of them are about what happens when you put a name on something, or when you learn some codified knowledge.

"Do you think 'the brain' is a good title for the brain?"

Good enough for me, I said. But clearly this wasn't an etymology question.

"Well, whatever you think your brain is," he persisted, "is that all there is? I doubt it. Everything that has a title has a fixed use, right? When we speak about 'the brain,' the brain I'm speaking about is what everyone is using to identify and learn what it is they think they like. That could be inspiration, education, whatever they call it. But the brain itself exists because it's the motor that causes you to be the human that you are. It doesn't necessarily mean that it's making you any better."

Though he is fascinated by music theory, he is suspicious of any enforced construct of thought. Standard Western harmony is the big dilemma, and particularly the fact that the notation for many instruments (including two of his three instruments—the alto saxophone and trumpet, but not the violin) must be transposed to fit the "concert key" of C in Western music.

Coleman talks about "music" with care and accuracy, but he talks about "sound" with love. He doesn't know how we will ever properly understand the power of notes when they are bossed around by the common Western system of harmony and tuning. "When you think of a minor seventh chord—E, G, B, and D— well, E-G-B is a minor chord, and G-B-D is a major chord," he observed. "The only note that's causing those two chords to have a different sound is D. What blows my mind is, how can intelligence be used to deceive what something is, and still be intelligence?"

Western harmony, in other words, is one of the fixed uses that bothers him so thoroughly.

Don't misunderstand; Coleman is not endorsing cacophony. He believes that making music is a matter of finding euphonious resolutions between different players. (And much of his music keeps referring to, if not actually staying in, a major key.) But the reason he appreciates Louis Armstrong, for example, is that he sees Armstrong as someone who improvised in a realm beyond his own knowledge. "I never heard him play a straight chord in root position for his idea," he said. "And when he played a high note, it was the finale. It wasn't just because it was high. In some way, he was telling stories more than improvising."

Coleman's first request was something by Josef Rosenblatt, the Ukrainian-born cantor who moved to New York in 1911 and became one of the city's most popular entertainers of any kind— as well as a symbol for not selling out your convictions. (He turned down a position with the Chicago opera company but was persuaded to take a small role in Al Jolson's film *The Jazz Singer*.) I brought him some recordings from 1916, and we listened to "Tikanto Shabbos," a song from Sabbath services. Rosenblatt's voice came booming out, strong and clear at the bottom, miraculous coloratura runs at the top.

"I was once in Chicago, about twenty-some years ago," Coleman told me. "A young man said, 'I'd like you to come by so I can play something for you.' I went down to his basement and he put on Josef Rosenblatt, and I started crying like a baby. The record he had was crying, singing, and praying, all in the same breath. And none of it was crossing each other. It was all separate. I said, 'Wait a minute. You can't find those notes. Those are not "notes." They don't exist.'"

He listened some more. Rosenblatt was working with text, singing brilliant figures with it, then coming down on a resolving note, which is confirmed and stabilized by a pianist's chord.

"I want to ask something," he said. "Is the language he's singing making the resolution? Not the melody. I mean, he's resolving. He's not singing a 'melody.'"

It could be that he's at least singing each little section in relation to a mode, I said.

"I think he's singing pure spiritual," he said. "He's making the sound of what he's experiencing as a human being, turning it into the quality of his voice, and what he's singing to is what he's singing about. We hear it as 'how he's singing.' But he's singing about something. I don't know what it is, but it's *bad*."

I wonder how much of it is really improvised, I said. Which up-and-down melodic shapes, and in which orders, were well practiced, and which weren't.

"Mm-hmm," he said. "I understand what you're saying. But it doesn't sound like it's going up and down; it sounds like it's going *out*. Which means it's coming from his soul."

I told him that I liked the way music can do this: make you feel that country and ethnicity and language are finally not such great limitations, since there are always things in it that you can respond to, whoever you are.

"Yeah, me too," he replied. "I have a tape here of myself playing with the musicians of Joujouka." It came from his trip to the Rif Mountains of Morocco in 1973. Small parts of these recordings appeared on his album *Dancing in Your Head,* but the raw tapes of Coleman playing with about thirty musicians, on drums and oboelike raitas, have not yet been released. Our listening to it violated my rule for these interviews: we must listen to no music that the interviewee participated in. But any rule begins to lose relevance around Coleman. Anyway, I wanted to hear one of the tapes.

It was electrifying: a massed, buzzing sound in no determinate key, with Coleman soloing passionately over it, in his own melodic language. "What's so amazing is that you can't enter that by notes," he said. "You can only be affected by how it's making you feel, and then you play that. You can't say, 'I know where they are. I know what it is.' You can only respond to how it affects you."

The idea of people playing together, I suggested, and making their lines entwine in not-so-strictly defined phrases, is something he feels especially close to.

"Oh, I'm trying to get liberated with that every day," he reflected. "Being a human, you cannot expose something that you've experienced personally and expect your environment to reward you. They don't know that maybe you just got it naturally. I taught myself what I know, and I've learned to read music and write it, but that doesn't make me Einstein, or anything.

"That's the one thing that I'm beginning to realize, the older I get," he continued. "For me it ain't gonna get no better, and it ain't gonna get worse. I have to choose where I think I am in relation to what I believe. Basically, the only thing that I believe, truly, is that there's only two destinations: one is life, and one is death. And it seems to me that when death dies, the world is gonna be incredible.

"But let's talk about life," he said, cheerily. "There must be something eternal that has existed before anything any other person could see or touch or smell. I'm not talking about the sky. The quality that we call *human* has never not existed. I mean, we say Adam and Eve, right? But whoever found Adam and Eve? It says that they existed," he said.

You can say they existed if you believe Genesis, I said. I found it strange that we were going in this direction.

"You mean, they may not exist?"

They may not exist.

"Do you think that your parents, if they hadn't conceived you, you wouldn't have existed?"

I do believe that.

"Why?"

I wouldn't have had a physical presence.

"Oh. All right. Everything around here has a physical presence." He gestured around the room. "But it ain't serving nothing. All you're doing that way is paying bills. We're talking about a quality that has to do with the creation of form."

I answered that even a possibility, an absence, can affect human lives.

"It's impossible for you never to have existed at all, because when you didn't know that you existed, you did exist. I'm sitting here speaking to you; humanly, we are alive and talking. But the quality that we're talking about, that quality doesn't have a beginning or end. It is never *not* existing. That's what I mean. And the sad part about it—this is really strange—is that, if it wasn't for women, there wouldn't be no people. But who put the woman in a position to do that? Did she put herself there? That don't make sense!"

You know that male seahorses carry the baby, I said.

"Oh, that's cold," he said.

When Coleman grew up in Fort Worth, he knew two saxophonists whom he talks about more than any others: Ben Martin and Red Connors. Both died young, and neither was recorded. Martin was an alto saxophonist, but it was the tenor player, Connors, who introduced Coleman to Charlie Parker.

Coleman grew up loving Parker and bebop in general. "It was the most advanced collective way of playing a melody and at the same time improvising on it," he said. Certainly, he was highly influenced by Parker's phrasing.

He saw Parker play in Los Angeles (which he pronounces "Los Angle-iss") in the early 1950s. "He didn't play any of the music that I liked that I'd heard on a record. He looked at his watch and stopped in the middle of what he was playing, stopped the band, put his horn in his case, and walked out the door. I said, *ohh*. I mean, I was trying to figure out what that had to do with music, you know? Basically, he had picked up a local rhythm section, and he was playing mostly standards. He mostly didn't play any bebop.

"It taught me something," he continued. "He knew the quality of what he could play, and he knew the audience, and he wasn't impressed enough by the audience to do something that they didn't know. He wasn't going to spend any more time trying to prove that."

We listened to "Cheryl," a Parker quintet track from 1947. "I was drawn to the way Charlie Parker phrased his ideas," he said. "It sounded more like he was composing, and I really loved that. Then, when I found out that the minor seventh and the major seventh was the structure of bebop music—well, it's a sequence. It's the art of sequences. I kind of felt, like, I gotta get out of this."

He talks a lot about sequences. (John Coltrane, he believes, was a good saxophone player who was lost to them.) Regarding his Parker worship, he kept the phrasing but got rid of the sequences. "I first tried to ban all chords," he said, "and just make music an idea, instead of a set pattern to know where you are. I'm at the point now where modulation is the closest thing to pure improvisation." Coleman has thoughts, of course, on how to define the ideal of pure improvisation. "No key, no rhythm, and no time," he quickly recited, like the answer in a catechism. "Just the idea itself. It's how you put it."

Ben Martin, that other big presence in Coleman's mind, seemed to get this. "With him, it was just the idea, not the execution on the horn. To this very day, that's the one thing that I'm very nervous about: the idea. The idea is not an environment. It's not an arrangement. It's not a key; it's not a chord. It's only the idea."

He suddenly posed another question. "Is the idea the only repetition that the brain allows you to function from?"

This word threw me. The only *repetition*?

"Yeah," he said. For instance, the other day I was rehearsing with my band here, and I was trying to figure out whether I can play ideas and still be where the band is," he said. "I realized it wouldn't work."

So the ideas he was talking about weren't structural, I ventured. They were spatial ideas, or textural ideas.

"Something like that," he replied. "I was telling my band, there's these three chords, and they have all twelve notes in them. I can show you that there's one note that couldn't enter any of those chords, because it would always be out of key. That *exists*. I can't be a church on all styles, but it seems that the 'idea' for music is not the improvised concept; it's more of a mathematical concept, like a whole step and a half step—like D, E, F, those three notes—a whole step and a chromatic. That, basically, is not an idea. It's a thought-out logic."

But he found that he had run into another riddle. "I started thinking, what is an idea?" he continued. "You can't have an idea if it doesn't correspond with the present information that you're using. Now, what is the difference between an idea and something that works?"

In essence, through this question, Coleman was arguing that a musical idea can be valid without imposing itself as an inviolate system.

You mean, I said, rephrasing the question, do all ideas have to work?

"Yeah," he said, "that's right, that's right."

Do all abstract ideas have to work?

"Yeah."

In music?

"The answer is no."

It is strange, Coleman's obsession with taxonomy, measurements, scales, church doctrine, all of which he calls unnatural. But why does he let it bother him at all? He proved early in his career that he could write beautiful melodies by ear. (Coleman didn't come to terms with standard music theory until about 1960.) Everybody's got some sort of system, and he does too. He phrases melodies a certain way; he mostly avoids minor tonality; he favors a certain upper-middle pitch range on his horn. People learn to play with him, and they can learn his tunes without sheet music. What's the problem? Why can't he just forget about what he has no use for? For instance, when he was rehearsing with the band, trying to play "ideas" and then realizing it just wouldn't work, what made him decide that it wouldn't?

"That's a very good question," he said. "When you say, 'what made you decide that it didn't work'—well, there's something in your mind, when you said that. You realized that there's something that could make it clear. That's why you asked. Well, I agree with you. That's a legitimate question. I don't have the answer. But I know why you asked the question. Let's assume that the reason why you asked me, and the reason why I don't have the answer, is the same."

This is the sound of Coleman's gate closing. He loves exposing you to his cast of mind, but if he senses you trying to pick it apart, or superimposing a grid of Western logic on it, he holds you at bay with a charming tautology.

When, about six months later, Coleman won a Grammy Award in the lifetime achievement category, a friend of mine shepherded him around Los Angeles for a few days. The night after Coleman's memorable acceptance speech—which began, "It really is very, very real to be here tonight in relation to life and death, and I'm sure they both love each other"—he faced a field of microphones at one of the backstage press rooms on his schedule. "Ornette," my friend counseled, "some reporters are going to ask you very fluffy questions now. You don't have to give them more than one-line answers. They don't want more."

"Ornette Coleman!" ventured one. "What is the achievement in your life that you are proudest of?"

He looked pensively at her. "I'm gonna have to go way back to answer that one," he said. "Way, way back. In fact, I'm gonna have to go back to the moment when you asked me that question." The interview stopped.

I had suggested listening to gospel music, and Coleman was enthusiastic. "It's a true sound of what people call the sinner trying to make peace with God," he said.

I brought something I felt he might like: a record of sacred harp music—white, rural, choral music, about a hundred voices, groups of them in loose unison. We listened to "The Last Words of Copernicus," written in 1869 and recorded by Alan Lomax in Fyffe, Alabama, in 1959.

"That's breath music," he said, as big groups of singers harmonized in straight eighth-note patterns, with plain voices but much character. "They're changing the sound with their emotions. Not because they're hearing something." But then we were off on another topic: the idea of whether a singer ought to seek a voicelike sound for his voice.

I tried another one: the Kyrgyzstani singer Zainidin Imanaliev, accompanying himself on the *komuz*, a three-stringed lute. He was singing a song called "Küidüm Chok," highly emotional and pitch-precise, with guitar patterns that inevitably, for Western listeners, recall the blues. You can't mistake what he's singing about: helpless love. (The last stanza, translated, sighs: "Like a blossoming silvery poplar/you walk coquettishly in a silvery scarf/unable to find a way to be with you/I am left suffering like a weeping young camel.")

"Mm!" Coleman responded. "You know what I realize? That all sound has a need. Otherwise it wouldn't have a use. Sound has a use. More than any other element. You use it to establish something— an invisible presence or some belief."

Here, as a kind of refrain, Imanaliev made the notes of his chest voice ascend and narrow into a high whistling tone—almost like Howlin' Wolf's howl. "Whew," Coleman said. "He's singing like he's a little kid. *Mmf*. But isn't it amazing that sound causes the idea to sound the way it is, more than the idea?"

Finally, the experiment broke down. It's hard to keep Coleman talking about anyone else's music. These mystical-logical puzzles are too interesting to him.

He still writes new pieces for each concert and was about to leave for some European shows. "Right now, I'm trying to play the instrument," he said, "and I'm trying to write, without any restrictions of chord, keys, time, melody, and harmony, but to resolve the idea eternally, where every person receives the same quality from it, without relating it to some person. I don't know what causes us to have an idea. But you can't learn what life is. It's already complete."

He told a childhood story about his mother, who, as he kept reminding me, was born on Christmas day. After he received his first saxophone, he would come to her after learning how to play something by ear. "I'd be saying, 'Listen to this! Listen to this!'" he remembered. "You know what she'd tell me? 'Junior, I know who you are. You don't have to tell me.'"

Set List

Cantor Josef Rosenblatt, "Tikanto Shabbos," from *The Great Cantors* (Pearl), recorded 1916.

Charlie Parker, "Cheryl," from *Best of the Complete Savoy & Dial Studio Recordings* (Savoy), recorded 1947.

Alabama Sacred Harp Singers, "The Last Words of Copernicus," from *Southern Journey,* vol. 9: *Harp of a Thousand Strings—All Day Singing from the Sacred Harp* (Rounder), recorded 1959.

Zainidin Imanaliev, "Küidüm Chok" (translation: "I Burn, I Smoulder Like Charcoal"), from *Music of Central Asia,* vol. 1: *Tengir-Too, Mountain Music of Kyrgyzstan* (Smithsonian Folkways), recorded 2004.

6

The Flying Modulation

Maria Schneider

Clipped to the music desk of Maria Schneider's upright piano, when I visited her, was a picture of the ballerina Sylvie Guillem. Spread out all over it were sketches for a new composition, "Cerulean Skies." It was an assignment for an event she was both looking forward to and dreading: a festival in Vienna programmed by the theater director Peter Sellars, celebrating the 250th anniversary of Mozart's birth.

It is a piece about the migration of birds, and Schneider had been struggling with it, trying to get the right quality of motion. When she composes, she often plays a sequence into a tape recorder, then gets up to play it back, and moves around the room to the phrases of the music, seeing how it feels when danced. "It helps me figure out where things are, and what needs to be longer," she said.

Much of Maria Schneider's large-ensemble jazz of the last six years has been nearly a figurative description of long-flow movement, particularly dancing or flying. And even when that's not what it's really about—as it is in her piece "Hang Gliding" or the various dances represented in her suite "Three Romances"—that's still, in a sense, what it's really about.

In her apartment on Manhattan's Upper West Side, Schneider—forty-five when I listened with her—composes at the piano; onstage she stands and conducts her band, which ranges from seventeen to twenty musicians. Judging herself a mediocre pianist, she doesn't play the instrument onstage; she is one of the few well-known jazz composers who do not perform with their own ensembles.

It is extremely unlikely in these times for a jazz composer who isn't also an instrumental star to keep a seventeen-piece band more or less intact for more than a decade. But she has managed it, since 1994, through grants and ambitious touring and, in more recent years, an innovative system of releasing recordings through the online label ArtistShare, which treats customers as "members," allowing them not only to preorder her new music at standard CD prices but, for a little more, to see how its various parts are coming together, via streaming-video updates.

That natural flowing sound in her music is not easily come by. "If you had talked to me last Friday"—we met on a Monday afternoon—"I would have burst into tears," she said. "It's so much work, I can't even tell you." She ran off a list of gigs she had coming up, on three different continents. "Everybody's a freelance musician, and for some reason, the stars didn't align this time. So I'm having some really brand-new people coming in—two that I've never even met. That means I have to *rehearse* all these different groups." Her voice was losing its composure.

* * *

Both the open-air sound of Schneider's music and its sense of hope and possibility make sense laid against the details of her life. She and her two sisters grew up in rural southwest Minnesota, in an agricultural town called Windom, 150 miles from Minneapolis.

"We had all these big picture windows," she said, "and you'd look out the window and you'd see nothin'." She smiled. Schneider is blond and slim, with large, deep-set eyes. When she talks about her art, or about music that she likes, her dry voice flushes and cracks, and she straightens her body or moves her limbs when she needs to express something. "When your entertainment isn't provided for you," she continued, "your life is full of fantasy."

As a girl, Schneider would play the piano and imagine that New York talent scouts might be driving nearby in cars with radio antennae that could pick up her music and discover her. "So I was always on," she explained, "prepared for one of these talent scouts."

Her father designed machinery for processing flax, and his company required him to get a pilot's license so he could fly to flax fields in Canada and North Dakota. He kept his plane in a hangar behind the family garage, and he would often take his daughter flying with him. "When you're in a small plane, and it banks—when the plane goes like this?" She turned her flat palm to a ninety-degree angle. "The earth looks perpendicular to the wing, and I used to look at the earth and think that we were straight. I didn't think we were tilted."

* * *

Schneider learned something about musical motion with Gil Evans, the great composer and arranger, who died in 1988. After attending the Eastman School of Music, she moved to New York and worked as his assistant, copying and transcribing. He never helped her directly with her music—she didn't presume to ask—but she has since become, in a sense, his best-known contemporary student. Her work has been frequently compared to his, which, she says, only suggests that his music isn't understood well enough. But it is an almost inescapable conclusion: Evans is her precedent, the impressionism-influenced jazz composer who recused himself as a pianist from some of his greatest work, created his own sound colors, and did not make typical "big band" jazz.

She put on "Concierto de Aranjuez," from *Sketches of Spain,* one of Evans's collaborations with Miles Davis. She had conducted it with her own band several times since Evans's death. It starts with castanets and harp; then soft orchestral lines move in for the theme, before Davis enters, a minute into the piece. "Check this out," she said.

Davis enters with a soft flourish, while the castanets trail on five more seconds after his entrance. ("The castanets shoulda quit sooner." She frowned. "That's how it was written.") It's an amazing piece of writing. Suddenly, a quiet forms around Davis, but not an empty one; the music around him goes into slow motion, and its colors seem to change.

"You know how Armani knows how to dress a woman up and make her look just incredible?" she asked. "Gil knew how to dress a soloist and make that soloist so beautiful, you know? So there's all this fluttering—this movement, the tuba's playing these melodies, there's all these things going on—and when Miles enters, everything stops."

As if stirring to life again, more lines form, with a curious momentum; they're not just notes but crossing trajectories, new instruments floating to the top of the arrangement. "What blows me away about Gil is the lines," she said. "There's always a line moving. He's so much like Ravel; everything's always moving. He can do these incredibly slow tempos, and there's a feeling of motion even in a slow tempo. There's always an expectation of a line moving."

But it must have made a big difference when he was conducting, I said. Wasn't it crucial that he himself made things more taut, made some lines trickle a little longer or shorter? He was a composer and conductor working with improvisers; he must have made changes on the spot. "Not necessarily," she said. "The lines are there. The bass and tuba are playing a melody, always. The bass is never relegated to just bass notes. It's all there; it's very tightly composed."

Schneider once conducted the piece from a transcription; then she did it again after Evans's original scores were found. She was amazed by the difference. "I saw everything in them, and that's when I realized: It's like a watch, where every little gear attaches to something else. The music and the soloist are an inseparable entity."

What's important to Schneider isn't just standing in front of a band and having it play her music, but setting up structures for the improvisers so that their phrasing becomes part of the music, which changes her subsequent writing. It has taken some time for this looping to work. I confess I used to have problems with her early music, finding it too pretty and a little rhythmically square. But later, once the band grew into itself, rhythm took over the music, and her writing became simpler and more mystical.

"I had a friend," she said, "who once asked Frank Foster, of the Basie band, 'How did you guys learn to phrase that way?' He said, 'I never thought about it.' I realized, that's how it happens: those particular people playing that music found that thing, and before you knew it, it was the 'Basie sound.' How did it happen? Nobody can really say how. It was through incremental shifts in feel, from night to night."

Her band evolved in a similar way, she figured. "It developed its own organic way of phrasing, which was the result of these particular people playing this particular music. And then, as a result of my hearing that phrasing, I start writing to that. They show me what's possible."

A similarly trusting approach applies to her method of making records. With a movie camera, or a digital audio recorder, Schneider documents each stage of a new piece of music, including recording sessions, even problematic ones. Then anyone can stream all that documentation from her Web site, mariaschneider.com, or from her page at ArtistShare's site.

This is quite an act of transparency for someone who comes across as anxious about the creative process, even compulsively disappointed in her own music; talking to her, you understand that art is about half agony. But the system seems to have worked.

Concert in the Garden, her first record with ArtistShare and also her first to use this artist-peeping technology, won a Grammy in 2005; sixteen months after our 2006 conversation, so did "Cerulean Skies," the bird-migration piece, in the 2007 awards. She believes that above all else the process proves that a good piece can result from unpromising beginnings.

So it's good for your attitude, I said.

"And it's good for others," she said, usefully. "For the world to pretend that art is so damn easy and logical—I just do this and this and it's fine—well, that's not the way it is," she chided. "I've given clinics before where I talk about my process and I say, 'I'm writing this piece now and it's so hard, and I don't know what I'm doing.' And I've had kids come to me, crying, *'I'm so relieved to hear you say that!'* Everybody feels so much pressure."

A curious fact of Schneider's working life is that she writes music of the solitary imagination yet has become a symbol of the jazz education movement, which tends to encourage teaching by imitation. In any case, clinics for young musicians regularly pop up on Schneider's schedule. Her career was started, she reckoned, by a commission she was awarded in 1990 by the International Association of Jazz Educators. Not long after that, her band was playing Monday nights at Visiones, the now-defunct New York City jazz club. The gigs led to more commissions, with European radio orchestras, the bread-and-butter of large-ensemble jazz composers. Thus could she quit her day job.

Given her own résumé, she has thought a lot about what jazz education can do for young musicians, and what it can't. "Some people think jazz education's a bad thing," she said. "The only bad thing is when jazz education leads the person before they've explored something themselves. I had to do a lot of exploring and floundering without a lot of help. When I left Eastman, I was very frustrated, feeling like I wanted to find my own voice. And I was a little bit paint-by-numbers. But in retrospect I look back and I see hints of who I would become."

You have to reject a lot before you have something lasting, I suggested. "Bob Brookmeyer helped me with this," she said, nodding. "He'd ask me questions like, 'Why is there a solo now?' I'd say, 'Because it's a jazz piece, because I wrote the first part of the tune, and now there's a little send-off.' He'd say, 'There should never be a solo until the only thing that can happen is a solo.' I never knew what that meant, but what I started to realize was that I had this template branded into my head of *bass line, chord, comping, melody, tune, send-offs*, like you were buying a modular unit, and you could change certain aspects of it, but they were going to go together something like this. I mean, you could move it to a different key, change the orchestration, but . . .

"Then I started questioning these modular units. There doesn't have to be anything. There are no modular units. It's music, it's ideas, it's sound, it's vibration," she concluded.

I asked if her students were troubled by the open-endedness that she espouses.

"It's very daunting. If anything's possible, where do you begin? You want to give them limitations so that they can produce something. When you can suddenly do everything, what do you do? We live in eclectic times; we can do anything. I mean, I'm sorry, but when Mozart was writing, it was sonata form, baby."

—

Even thirty years ago, there didn't seem to be so many options. "Exactly. It's rough. So, that's where you have to find your own geometry, your own world," she said. "Look at Elliott Carter. He writes intensely complex music. But he has his own logic, his own technique. It's a world of math that resonates with him. I believe that for him it's intuitive. But trying to make me write a twelve-tone piece is like trying to ask me to write a beautiful piece in Portuguese. Everybody has to find their own language."

During the 1980s, the Adagio movement of Ravel's Piano Concerto in G Major fell on Schneider like a cash register from the sky. The piece overwhelmed her senses; she had to force herself to stop listening to it. She still thinks it is "the most gorgeous piece of music on the planet," and would like it played at her funeral. She feels it so deeply that her reactions to Martha Argerich playing it, with the Berlin Philharmonic, were much more physical than cerebral.

As the slow, lovely opening unfolded in its three-beat rhythm, she made low, murmuring noises. "Mmm. The harmony." The piano played a short trill, and the flutes entered. She closed her eyes. "It's just like a breeze." The strings drifted in. Then, almost four minutes in, a gently dissonant four-note piano figure changes the temperature of the music. "I mean, talk about blues notes, but used in a new way. Unh! *Uhhh!* It's such angularity, but such *beauty*. It kills me. Have you ever seen the Jerome Robbins choreography to this?"

The dissonant piano line emerged again. "That is so unbelievable. It's like a seventh over the third, and then a sharp-nine,

I think. It's basically blues." The orchestra came to a consonant rest. Suddenly agitated, Schneider got up out of her chair. "And in this part, Kyra Nichols, when she dances in the New York City Ballet, she has this little skirt, and she starts doing, you know, pas de bourrée around the stage, and then she's just dancing around as if the wind is blowing and it's just like UNNNH! It's to die."

We listened to the end, through all the symmetrical rising and falling in the piece. "It has this sense of motion, the timing of motion," she said. She appeared to be searching for new words, then decided these really were the apt ones. "When that piece begins, it just breathes. It leaves you feeling just *settled*. And then there are these little tensions in it that just make you squeeze one muscle a little bit. The harmony starts to move, and things start to drop out, and it creates this incredible momentum. By the end, when the strings are coming in, it's just . . . there's so much *motion*."

But Schneider was also caught up in how the moving pieces interacted and developed. "He creates a sense of motion with harmony, the slightest tension between the melody and the harmony, and it's like, if you bring two elements and they push apart—that creates motion," she explained. "If things are too settled all the time and too consonant all the time, it leaves you rested. So he just slowly plays on the tension. Just like in life, sometimes, boy, time goes by really fast, and it's just a ride. And sometimes, every minute is just *excruciating* because you're being forced through issues. He has this way of forcing you slightly through little *issues*.

"And then," she added, "it's just so *beautiful*. It feels so pure and kinda naive at the same time. It just feels totally honest, in the way that Portela feels honest."

The turnaround moment for her band was the album *Allegresse*, from 2000. Around that time her music lost some of its academic stuffiness and its obsession with vertical harmony. Part of this, she explained, was a result of her having spent time in Brazil in 1998. "I was going through tough times in my life," she said. "When we landed in Rio and I saw the landscape, I knew my life was going to change."

She put on a track called "A Maldade Não Tem Fim," from an album by Velha Guarda da Portela, the dynastic group formed by the elders of the Portela samba school, which competes annually in Rio's carnival. Typical of its kind, the song has a bright, huge melody; a trombone plays over the mandolinlike *cavaquinho* and the tambourinelike *pandeiros*; a male voice (Armando Santos's) sings the verses scratchily, a thunder of voices joining in on the chorus.

During her first visit to Rio, she explained, the composer Paolo Moura took her to a rehearsal at the samba school he belongs to, Imperatriz Leopoldinense. Samba-school rehearsals are like organized parties, held in warehouses, at the edge of favela neighborhoods; there are hundreds of percussion instruments playing together. (Once I visited a rehearsal of Mangueira, another Rio samba school; it was the loudest and most provocative sound I had ever heard.) It suggested to Schneider some new ideas about music's functions.

"What I love in Brazilian music," Schneider said, "is that the way they're singing is *sustenance*. It's not about making music either for entertainment or for the conservatory—you know, music is here"—she spread her hands apart—"and your life is here. Life and music are one. The music I love is necessary for life, for survival.

"Flamenco—it makes living possible. Blues and early jazz—it made living possible. Samba is like alchemy. It turns pain into joy, into magic. My music was very intense and serious and very jazz, even though it was influenced by classical music. But after that, my priorities changed," she said. "I really didn't care if my music impressed anybody anymore, or if it was complex."

When she got home from Rio, she didn't immediately start writing in the style of samba. She began borrowing rhythm, loosely, from the more jazz-influenced *choro* style of Brazilian music. Later she moved toward flamenco, with its 12/8 buleria rhythm. She has since become obsessed with the accordion as a new voice in her ensemble; to several pieces she has added a *cajón*, the percussive wooden box of Peruvian music, and she hasn't written with swing rhythm since.

She is still a jazz composer, by self-identification, working with jazz improvisers. But the music is pulling farther away from any sort of conventional jazz.

"Sometimes I feel like, in the world of jazz, people think that more chromaticism all the time is going to make their music hipper," she said disappointedly. "It's like, no. Music is a time-oriented art. So it's how you play a person's attention through time.

"I mean, here and there you'll capture an experience in jazz that just makes you go . . ." She opened her eyes wide and gasped. "But to me it happens less and less, and I think that's because musicians think they have to keep playing more and more. Sometimes I leave those clubs and come home and listen to Bach cello suites. One line. Some space around one note. Or nothing. Nothing for weeks on end."

Finally she wanted—really wanted—to hear "Up, Up and Away," the hit by the Fifth Dimension, written by Jimmy Webb. It entered her bloodstream when she was a girl, she said. During the first lyric line ("Would you like to ride in my beautiful balloon?"), Schneider cocked a finger.

"Now check this out," she said. "Modulation, up a minor third. That's the flying modulation. It's all over my new music." She mentioned a few of her songs that contained similar modulations: "Hang Gliding," "Coming About."

"And now: up another minor third." (The Fifth Dimension was singing, "For we can flyyy . . .") "Now it's going down—let's see—a major third. And you hear the flutes?" (They appeared after the line "It wears a nicer face in my beautiful balloon.") "That's Gil Evans, I'm sorry." (The arrangements were by Marty Paich, a West Coast jazz arranger and a contemporary of Evans.)

She seemed self-conscious about praising an AM radio tune from her childhood in terms that should be reserved for Major Works of Art. But she raved: "Jimmy Webb is a genius. That tune modulates six times, if not more. Ah. I get chills. Am I crazy? Who could *dare* to write that? It modulates as much as 'Giant Steps' does," she said, referring to the John Coltrane composition, of which she wrote her own revised arrangement. "I mean, 'Giant Steps' is just moving by major thirds; what's the difference?"

Motion, flying, nostalgia; it seems important, this thing about flying in your father's plane, I said, a little embarrassed by the obviousness of the psychology.

To my surprise, she grew excited. "Maybe because of the motion! The openness and the motion," she said. "I never thought about it."

She thought about it.

"But also there's the bird thing," she added. "We had birds, we had a pet goose, we had crows. My mother used to set the wings of birds and stuff. We had a house full of animals.

"The goose never learned to fly, but the goose used to fly with my dad, in the plane. The crows were free, but unfortunately, when they were little, before they were imprinted, they fell out of a nest. So they were free to fly all over town, but eventually the police made us lock them up because they were a public disturbance."

How? I said. By pecking?

"They'd sit on the telephone wires, and the dogs would bark at them. They learned to bark, so they'd bark back. And then, in the winter, the crow cage, which was huge, was kept down at the plant, and the night watchman taught them to say 'go to hell.' So these birds would come out in the spring and say 'go to hell.' My childhood was surreal."

Set List

Miles Davis with Gil Evans, "Concierto de Aranjuez," from *Sketches of Spain* (Columbia), recorded 1959.

Maurice Ravel, Piano Concerto in G Major, Martha Argerich with the Berlin Philharmonic, from *Prokofiev, Ravel: Piano Concertos* (Deutsche Grammophon), recorded 1967.

Velha Guarda da Portela, "A Maldade Não Tem Fim," from *Portela Passado Na Gloria* (RGE), recorded 2002.

Fifth Dimension, "Up, Up and Away," from *Greatest Hits on Earth* (Arista), recorded 1972.

7

You've Got to Finish Your Thought

Bob Brookmeyer

To those listening closely, Bob Brookmeyer, the trombonist and composer, has become both the mature conscience and the hectoring elder of contemporary jazz. A fine and fizzy improviser in his youth, with a fascination for bebop and Kansas City jazz, he is now known for late-period writing that deals with the truculent and complicated emotions of living, and for raging in interviews against business-as-usual in the jazz world. Yet Brookmeyer has largely absented himself from that world.

He lives in Grantham, New Hampshire, with his wife, Jan, and when we got together in 2006 he was composing long-form pieces commissioned by European jazz orchestras, in his basement studio, which overlooks a wooded slope. He was also bearing up well—with a mixture of general cynicism and specific tenderness toward the people he loves—in a long battle with lymphoma.

Jazz trombonists can be odd or antic people; it's something to do with the smeariness of the instrument's sound, the ungainliness of its size, the pathos of its second-class status in jazz. Brookmeyer is more than that, almost Lear-like. Six foot three with an actor's baritone, he is candidly boastful about his own brilliance as a musician but insecure about his place as a composer; he is a recovering alcoholic with unresolved regret and anger about many things, from his country's foreign policy to his childhood.

Brookmeyer's close listeners include his students and colleagues in jazz education, as he has become a kind of guru at the New England Conservatory; those who knew him as a brilliant foil in Stan Getz's popular quintets of the 1950s or as the formidable intellect of Gerry Mulligan's Concert Jazz Band and the Thad Jones–Mel Lewis Orchestra in the early and mid-1960s; and the dedicated ones who seek out his newer work, despite the fact that he is seldom invited to perform it in America. (There is so little demand for it—as he will be the first to tell you—that he doesn't have a booking agent.)

The first track on his 2006 album, *Spirit Music*, recorded with his largely European, eighteen-piece band, the New Art Orchestra, is called "The Door." It begins almost primevally, with a gravitas rarely encountered in jazz. First there is a single, deep, sustained tone, played on synthesizer and piano. It lasts for a full minute before leading into two seesawing chords among four trombones and five woodwinds, an E minor and a D minor. After that, the record keeps opening up different vistas, areas of tightly written, color-sensitive arrangements.

Brookmeyer is the composer and conductor of the music, and only occasionally takes a trombone solo, such as on the track "Alone"; with his first notes, a dark jollity suddenly enters the picture, a well of accumulated life experience. His sound is broad and

emotional, roomy enough for old-fashioned song and tonal abstraction. His music sounds tense and stubborn and extremely tender; his
talk, too, falling out in complete paragraphs, is full of these tempers.

He does not give up easily, though at various times he has been
tempted. In his forties, while living in Los Angeles and working in
recording studios, he reached a protracted bottom point with al-
coholism, almost dying from it. Soon after, in his fifties, he nearly
quit jazz altogether to become a classical composer. Along the
way, he has wondered whether his time would be better spent as a
counselor to alcoholics.

Born in Kansas City, Missouri, in 1929, Brookmeyer endured an
unhappy early youth that coincided with the high period of
Kansas City swing, when Count Basie was the North Star. He first
heard Basie at the Tower Theater in 1941, on a Sunday matinee in
between showings of western movies, with his father.

"I melted," he declared, in his low, rumbling voice. "It was the
first time I felt good in my life. I was not a very successful child.
This was the first body thrill I ever had. I just said, 'Oh, my God,
I've got to do this.' It completely overwhelmed me. I went back
several times."

Sitting in his studio, surrounded by piles of CDs, we first listened to Basie's "9:20 Special," from 1941, and his hearing clamped
on to the piece's details, particularly the ensemble work. "You hear
the sax background?" he remarked, under Buck Clayton's trumpet
solo. But when it came to Basie's own contribution, he had too
much to say. We stopped the piece to talk.

"New Orleans was a whole other feel, but Kansas City was concentrating on the smooth, rhythmic 4/4," he said. "That was

everything. There was what you might call a *coolness*—that's an awful word—a subtlety, and a strength that didn't hit you over the head." This applied to rhythm sections, too. "*Long* beats on the bass. Drums really concentrating on cymbals, making a smooth patina."

Basie himself was key to all this. "He had supernatural powers," Brookmeyer said. "He didn't evince a lot of effort. Whereas other people seemed to take music and pound it into the ground—or bounce it off the earth—Basie came from under the crust of the earth and through your feet."

Talking about Basie led him back to the story of his own maturation. "My mother and my father were both teachers, and the Depression wiped them out." His father reinvented himself as an accountant, but Brookmeyer was closer to his mother.

"There was kind of a gang of two, my mother and I against him. There would be quarrels during dinner, and I'd get up and leave the table, say, 'The hell with this,' and go for a walk. Also, for some reason, I was mistreated in grade school. Beaten, insulted by strangers. For some reason I didn't fit in.

"It got better later on when I was in music. We moved to a better neighborhood and a better school, and I could now play trombone in a dance band. I was, sort of, somebody. I got pledged to a fraternity, and all that nonsense. But the early damage was done. So music saved my life.

"Hearing Basie gave me a direction. We were friends. Amazing, that a little trombone player from Kansas City could be a friend of Bill's. I got to play with him one time—at Town Hall, with Coltrane, Pepper Adams, Art Taylor, and George Duvivier."

How did it feel to be playing in a small band with Basie? "It was like the first feeling I had when I was eleven, only you add twenty tons of cocaine. I could understand now, finally, viscerally, how the other guys in the band felt playing with him.

"But, my one regret . . . ," he said. "I never wrote him a letter. About two years before he died, I wanted to write him a letter, and tell him how much he meant to me.

"I did write Dizzy a letter and thanked him, because Dizzy was very kind to me," he continued. "I'm trying to make that a habit— to write to people in and out of music that have meant a lot to me. I'm getting ready to write my third one now, to a friend of mine, a priest in California, who's getting old."

A year after Brookmeyer's Basie epiphany, Charlie Parker left Kansas City, about to help invent bebop, and jazz changed. Brookmeyer was working in the city's black clubs, first as a trombonist at age fifteen, then as a pianist at seventeen. "Kansas City was so segregated that I didn't know it was segregated," he remarked. "We lived six blocks away from a black section, on the other side of Prospect Avenue. I drove down Prospect to get downtown, and I'd be passing black churches and gospel music—which left a very strong impression on me. When I began to play in clubs, I was getting to the point where they thought I might try to drink. So I was not really welcome, but in the black section I was. Often, professionally, I was the only white guy in the band."

Parker made his first significant bebop records in New York City, and these were critical for a young musician to absorb. Brookmeyer listened to them repeatedly at 16 RPM, on a navy-surplus phonograph, transcribing Parker's lines by ear.

The exercises did him good. "At that stage of the game," he said, "bebop was such a distant language, that what I learned, I owned." But he preferred to play in swing bands. "They were more fun for me," he explained. "Some of the beboppers played very well, but they seemed to imitate the worst parts of progress: heroin, bad attitudes, cliquishness." (He was also viewed as a square, he suspects, once he started attending the Kansas City Conservatory of Music.)

In 1951, he endured six months of army service in Columbia, South Carolina, under the scorn of an officer who looked unkindly on aesthetes in general, particularly white ones with black friends. Trying to defend himself, Brookmeyer recalled, he was publicly dressed down for being prone to "homosexual fits."

"The upshot," he continued, with acid relish, "was that my last three months in the army, I was 'gay,' with two friends who were black, and—ha *ha!*—I was a *musician*."

He was given an honorable discharge.

Back in Kansas City, he found a job with Tex Beneke's orchestra, which eventually led him to New York City. "I had to go to New York," he said. "I was getting nibbles. Stan Kenton called when I was asleep. My mother said, 'By the way, Stan Kenton called last night.' I said, 'What did you tell him?' She said, 'I told him you were asleep.' I thought, *I gotta get out of this place*."

By then Brookmeyer had switched to the valve trombone—a variation on the instrument's better-known form, with valves instead of a slide. (It has been his principal instrument ever since; the piano has returned only off and on.) He worked with Stan Getz in various small groups, and in 1953 took Chet Baker's place in Gerry Mulligan's quietly intricate quartet and sextet for a few years.

At the time, he basically idolized only tenor saxophonists, not trombonists. Lester Young represented his ideal. The only exception was Bill Harris, who played valve trombone in Woody Herman's orchestra. Harris influenced Brookmeyer's decision to move toward that instrument in 1948. "I didn't want to play slide trombone in the first place," he grumped. "Who wants to play slide trombone? If I had a kid who wanted to play slide trombone, I'd ground him for a year. Play piano, play saxophone. Anyway, I couldn't do what I wanted on slide trombone. I sounded like Bill Harris. If I played slide trombone now, I'd sound like a combination of Earl Swope and Bill Harris, drunk."

Harris disguised himself for the normal world with horn-rimmed glasses and a light mustache; he looked like a midlevel bank functionary. He was a brilliant, natural musician, a practical joker, and an alcoholic. According to legend, he once checked into a hotel after a gig by driving his car up the steps and into the lobby.

"I was in love with Bill Harris," Brookmeyer remembered. "He was, hands down, my hero. He got a plastic mouthpiece; I got a plastic mouthpiece. First time I saw him live was down at the municipal auditorium [in Kansas City]. I stood in front of the band for the first set, just staring at him. I'm walking around during intermission, and PoPsie [Randolph], the band boy, was taking Bill out to the bus, 'cause Bill would get drunk.

"I think it had to have been strange for Bill," he added, sympathetically, thinking about how he quickly eclipsed him on their shared instrument. "I came to New York and three years later I was placing second to J. J. Johnson in the [*Down Beat* magazine] polls, and Bill was way down there somewhere."

As with Basie, Brookmeyer never got to know Bill Harris well or tell him how much he liked him, and this has become a source of acute regret. "Man-to-man emotion was pretty scripted back then," he explained. "Men didn't say 'I love you' to each other until '65 or '70."

These furtive role models meant a lot to Brookmeyer, who was looking not just for musical guidance but for a sort of rule book about how to be an adult. "When you get early success after a failed early childhood," Brookmeyer said, "you're told by the world, 'You're successful, you know what you need to know.' Inside I was five years old; I always had to ask people, 'How do you do that?'" But outside of specific musical matters, "you couldn't emulate Bill," Brookmeyer said, plainly. "He actually traveled with a mannequin, when he was with Woody's band. He had a fourth-trombone seat, for the mannequin. This is a man who had very loose boundaries on what was permissible."

Brookmeyer chose a 1952 live version of "Lady Be Good," performed by one of Harris's small groups, a quintet including Eddie "Lockjaw" Davis on tenor saxophone. Harris's improvisation is extravagantly musical, bursting with melody—forcefully, he yanks it out of the instrument—in a tangle of swing and blues and bebop phrases.

Harris had an overpowering voice on his own, I said. Was he too large a presence for a big band, too disruptive?

"I wouldn't say disruptive," Brookmeyer corrected. "He was influential. His sound was highly emotional. His personality was so strong that he guided the band a lot. As a trombonist in a big band, you're in the middle of everything. You learn how things are made. My old joke is that saxophonists get all the girls, trumpet players make all the money, and trombone players develop an interior life."

* * *

In the 1960s, Brookmeyer's ambitions began to struggle against the conventions of jazz, the aspects of composition or improvisation or performance he has come to call, with derision, "rituals." Increasingly he turned to composing. "Playing is easy for me," he said. "It's fun. It's a nice hobby. I can pretty well turn it on and off. I can't do that with writing. A blank piece of paper is a great leveler."

What interested him most was overturning the consensual hierarchies in jazz. For a while, in the early 1960s, he played with the Jimmy Giuffre Trio—Giuffre on clarinet, Brookmeyer on trombone, and Jim Hall on guitar. They wanted to write music that balanced composition and improvisation, each crisscrossing with the other. Giuffre was interested in American themes—music that evoked big spaces, dance-band ritual, and spiritual loneliness—and Brookmeyer was perfect for him, bringing his Kansas City blues and mother-wit to the project. The record *Western Suite*, especially, functions outside of jazz's prescripted boxes.

His work later that decade for the Thad Jones–Mel Lewis band—such as his own canonized "ABC Blues," which used a twelve-tone row over blues changes—was intellectually rigorous. But when he returned to the band as its musical director, after a decade in Los Angeles that ended in two hospital rehabs, he really started pushing the band to its limits.

He had quit drinking for good and changed his musical focus. He was studying composition with Earle Brown, the modern classical music composer. "I kept meeting these classical composers who were jazz fans," he said, uncomprehendingly. "I found that depressing." He became interested in the most aggressive kinds of modern music—"music to make your teeth hurt," as he put it. He set about crafting pieces for the Mel Lewis Jazz Orchestra (Thad Jones had left by then) in which, as he explained, "solos became the background to the background."

This was an idea he first woke up to while arranging and composing for Gerry Mulligan's Concert Jazz Band in the early 1960s. "I realized that the soloists were necessary to add decoration to the backgrounds, because the backgrounds were really swinging," he said. "That could be an idea from Kansas City; Basie's band had great backgrounds." In short, he believed that the theme-solos-theme construction of the standard jazz piece had become normative and dull. Instead, he wanted to experiment with making solos secondary to ensemble passages. This was a major reversal, which would influence Maria Schneider and Jim McNeely, two current composers for large-ensemble jazz.

Back in New York in the early 1980s—which was also when he started his teaching career in earnest—he began to question the entire established language of jazz performance, but especially solos, which he had come to regard as "ritual gone mad." "My first rule became: the first solo only happens when absolutely nothing else can happen," he explained. "You don't write in a solo until you've completely exhausted what you have to say. If you give a soloist an open solo for thirty seconds, he plays like he's coming from the piece that you wrote. Then he says, 'What the hell was that piece that I was playing from?' And the next thirty seconds is, 'Oh, I guess I'll play what I learned last night.' And bang! Minute two is whoever he likes. Which is probably Coltrane." (When Brookmeyer talked about Coltrane, he growled; he admired his musicianship but hated the form his influence took on others.)

He developed a severe impatience with the jazz band's predictable workplace routine. He proposed evenings of music that would overturn the basic rituals of jazz-club presentation and decorum. People approaching the Village Vanguard on Seventh Avenue would pass actors and jugglers; once inside the club, music would come at them from all sides. "Someone's in the kitchen, playing," he imagined it. "Someone else is playing in the bathroom, someone in the hallway—not listening to each other, but each playing music I wrote, music with instructions."

This never actually came to pass. But Brookmeyer's last two pieces for the Thad Jones–Mel Lewis band were indeed semitheatrical, involving composed sections in which musicians turned to each other and talked. He finally left the band in 1981, after two years. "I wrote myself out of the band," he said.

One of his heroes at the time was Witold Lutoslawski, the Polish composer. In the early 1980s, he bought all of Lutoslawski's available records and scores; he dreamed of becoming his student. A friend of his, the jazz singer Nancy Harrow, found out the name of the composer's assistant and sent a message to Lutoslawski on Brookmeyer's behalf. A telegram eventually arrived at Brookmeyer's house, reading, "Witold Lutoslawski awaits your call."

"I had the number on my desk, and I waited three weeks," Brookmeyer remembered. I finally called, and thank God it was busy. I would have sounded like a three-year-old."

It's strange to hear you say that, I said. Look at whom you've worked with!

He frowned. "Yeah, but this is a whole other world. This is a world that's sophisticated and skilled beyond my wildest dreams."

We listened to Lutoslawski's *Cello Concerto,* a nearly twenty-five-minute piece finished in 1970, as performed by Mstislav

Rostropovich. It begins with a series of short D's played by the solo cello; after some side roads and confrontations between the cello and the orchestra, the repeated note comes back.

"Interested?" Brookmeyer said, grinning. A little later, the woodwinds and harps go up and down, in thirds. "It's *so* lovely, and so subtle," he enthused. "It's like a rainbow shooting up. That gets compressed into a chord, later on. And becomes a melody, also. He uses material that's so beautiful, and makes it happen again, so he raises expectations."

Slowly and repeatedly, the piece opens up new areas of sound and timbre. "The stagecraft is great," Brookmeyer said. "He referred to himself as a stage director rather than a conductor. He doesn't make mistakes, theatrically. I mean, the cello on the high A, sobbing at the end? The piece is supposed to be a good guy–bad guy thing, where the cello's the good guy and the band is the bad guy. It's a battle, somehow, and obviously the cello ascends and wins."

Brookmeyer talked about the qualities of music that are important to him. "How do you begin to speak to the listener?" he asked. "The listener doesn't have to like the process, but he needs to be in the process, to make the trip with you.

"In the eighties," he continued, "I began to wonder how long I could extend my musical thought and still not break the relationship with the listener, not put the listener to sleep. When I became a teacher, I realized that everybody writes too short. You've got to finish your thought. If you're gonna take a chance, take a chance on being boring." He added, quickly, "This is as a composer. Not as a soloist. Many young composers, under sixty, worry about being boring. But you'd be surprised; the listener wants to know who you are, where you're coming from."

His new music for large ensembles doesn't make anyone's teeth hurt. (He gives Jan, his fourth wife, some credit for cooling him out.) But he still has a problem with solos, even in his own orchestra, his continual source of pride. "Musicians will go on for hours and ruin a piece and make it boring; they have no idea how to play *from* the piece," he complained.

He watched me as I tried to think of a way to disprove his point. "I'm right," he said, evenly. "I'm very careful in my band who I give solos to. I never think about a soloist when I'm writing a piece. I just think about the piece and say, 'Okay, maybe it would be a good place to have a little release.'"

Brookmeyer's advice to jazz composers: *Keep your hand on the soloist, somehow—with long tones, chords, punches. Keep your hand on him, because he needs it.*

Set List

Count Basie Orchestra, "9:20 Special," from *America's Number One Band* (Sony Legacy), recorded 1941.

Bill Harris, "Lady Be Good," from *Live at Birdland, 1952* (Baldwin Street Music), recorded 1952.

Witold Lutoslawski, *Cello Concerto*, performed by Mstislav Rostropovich (EMI), recorded 1974.

8

Head of a Dog

Bebo Valdés

The Cuban pianist Bebo Valdés, a living repository of the glories of twentieth-century Cuban music, lives with his wife, Rose Marie, in a small ground-floor apartment in Brandbergen, Sweden, just outside of Stockholm. Around the place is an index to his remarkable life.

Valdés, tall and bold-featured, stands in a suit on the cover of a book published in Havana in the 1950s for the English-language market, *Cha Cha Cha & Mambo for Small Dance Bands*. The book sits on a shelf of well-thumbed sheet-music books: *100 of the Greatest Easy Listening Hits*, the Beatles, and the two volumes of Joseph Schillinger's *System of Musical Composition* books, the dense works valued by composers in the 1940s and '50s that break down melody, harmony, and rhythm into mathematic logic. Paintings by Haitian artists hang on the walls. Other objects haven't lived here as long: a Grammy and a key to the city of Madrid.

* * *

Slavery was abolished in Cuba in 1884. Bebo Valdés was born in 1918. His mother came from a Spanish family; his paternal grandfather was a slave. Afro-Cuban jazz is the ultimate mixture of African, European, and New World culture; as an example, it puts the *batá,* the two-headed drum of Yoruban religious music, alongside European harmony and American swing. But Valdés remembers a time when it was effectively prohibited to use the *batá* in a dance orchestra. He was the first to do so, in 1952.

That was at the club Tropicana, the biggest nightclub in Havana, where Valdés was the pianist in the house orchestra, during the height of the mambo's popularity. I asked him how it had come about, to put the *batá* into dance music. He shrugged. "Roderico Neyra, the choreographer of the club," he said, winding up, "had African-themed shows in November, December, January. He said, 'Why don't you write something that isn't just all drums?' It had been used orchestrally, in the symphonies of Obdulio Morales and Gilberto Valdés. But I was the first to use the *batá* in dance music."

I knew a little about Gilberto Valdés as a distant historical figure. A classical-music composer, he presented Afro-Cuban-influenced compositions at Havana's Municipal Theater in 1937, taking a stand against cultural prejudices. But Bebo Valdés—no relation to Gilberto—knew Gilberto Valdés as a person. "Gilberto Valdés was white, blond-haired and blue-eyed, and yet he was the best composer of African music around," he marveled. "What's the name of that American who wrote 'Yesterdays'? Jerome Kern, right. He was like Jerome Kern."

He turned to the piano, for the first of many demonstrations. "I want to explain a pentatonic scale," he said. He played a full

C-major scale and then omitted the fourth and seventh scale degrees, the F and the B, making it pentatonic. Then he used those notes to pick out the melody of Kern's "Old Man River." "I have forgotten some of this!" He laughed. "But that scale, that pentatonic scale, is based on African music."

Bebo Valdés graduated from Havana's Conservatorio Municipal in 1943. "It was the poor man's conservatory, and the best," he insisted. A gifted arranger, he worked with his hero, Ernesto Lecuona—probably the greatest Cuban composer of the century—toward the end of the older man's life, in the mid-1940s.

Valdés was in the inner circle of musicians that developed the mambo, along with the multi-instrumentalist Orestes López and the bassist Israel "Cachao" López. At the Tropicana—where he was also musical adviser—he played with, or arranged music for, most of Cuba's star singers and musicians, including Beny Moré (who sang for the club's orchestra), Miguelito Valdés, and Chano Pozo. When Nat King Cole, a habitué of the Tropicana, came to Havana to record his Spanish-language record *Cole Español*, Bebo Valdés played the piano and arranged the album. He was a one-stop paragon of playing and arranging, the epicenter of a thriving world.

He had five children in Cuba, including Chucho Valdés, who has gone on to become one of the greatest pianists in the world. In 1960, after the revolution, Bebo Valdés fled the country—landing in Mexico, where he worked in television and in recording studios and arranged for bolero singers, such as the very popular Lucho Gatica. He then moved on to Spain, where he became music director for the record label Hispavox. At a stop in Stockholm on a European tour with a group called Lecuona's Cuban Boys, he met and fell in love with Rose Marie Pehrson. He was forty-four and she was eighteen. He stuck around.

It was 1963. He would have liked to relocate to New York City, but his sister, who had moved there, warned him against the United States; he was, after all, a black man with a white wife. For a while he bided his time. He remembers being of the common opinion, while he was in Mexico, that Castro would not last three months.

But Valdés has never returned to Cuba. He stayed in Stockholm, starting a new family and playing piano in hotel lounges for more than thirty years. (Hence the easy-listening songbooks.) He has a working musician's pride, and no regrets; he is happy with all that he knows.

In 1994, the Cuban jazz saxophonist Paquito D'Rivera called, inviting him to Germany, to work on a record together. It was to be a loose, jam-session record, but Valdés wanted structure. He orchestrated nine of his own songs for a nonet in two days. And it was going to be a D'Rivera record, but it ended up as *Bebo Rides Again*, his first record in three decades.

In 2000, he took part in *Calle 54*, Fernando Trueba's documentary film about Latin jazz. Valdés's imposing wisdom and the lightness of his demeanor gave his scenes, and the movie as a whole, a kind of magic lift. Trueba, not satisfied to close that chapter, formed a record label with the film-and-music historian Nat Chediak and made a series of records involving Valdés. One of them, *Lágrimas Negras*, a record of boleros by Valdés and the Spanish gypsy singer Diego El Cigala, sold nearly a million copies, mostly in Europe. In Madrid and Barcelona, particularly, crowds started to applaud him on the street.

Since then he has kept moving, making a run of albums including

Bebo De Cuba, a double-disc that won a Grammy and a Latin Grammy in 2005; it included his original "Suite Havana." He toured the world with Cigala in 2004 and played a sold-out week of duo shows with the bassist Javier Colina at the Village Vanguard in late 2005, at the age of eighty-seven. What a remarkable late chapter.

Valdés was to turn eighty-eight shortly after I visited him. I came to his house in Stockholm with Chediak, the producer for Calle 54 records, to whom Valdés has become extremely loyal. Valdés is cheerful and punctual—so much so that his tour with Cigala thoroughly stretched his patience. (Cigala tends not to show up on time.) He and Rose Marie live not far from their two Swedish-born sons, Rickard and Raymond, whom he dotes on.

Valdés takes small steps, and moves quickly, especially toward his piano. He scoffed witheringly when asked about arthritis, and claimed to be never tired. ("And I'm not bragging," he added.) He practices scales and arpeggios for thirty minutes daily and prefers to eat one meal, around lunchtime. He does not dance well and seems to take a kind of pride in this fact. He does not drink alcohol—though he noted that he would take a sip when *"Lágrimas Negras"* is certified a million sold—but takes in prodigious amounts of American coffee throughout the day.

He speaks mostly in Spanish, but with sprays of Swedish and English, depending on whom he's talking to. (His son Rickard, who plays percussion in a Stockholm salsa band, finally learned Spanish in his midthirties.) His memory for names and dates is sharp, and for my visit, he prepared a precise list of music to listen to, each piece keyed to particular fascinations.

* * *

The first was his hero, Lecuona, who died in 1963. We heard Lecuona himself play "La Paloma," which stitches two-beat and three-beat rhythms together; Lecuona plays it with pronounced rhythmic shifts. It has the beauty of the French formal dances that originally accompanied slave masters when they moved from Haiti to Cuba in the nineteenth century. "I first heard of Lecuona when I was in conservatory, in 1934," he said. I asked if Lecuona's music was taught in conservatories back when Valdés was a student. "Oh, no, no," he said, surprised by the idea. "Only classical. Everything we learned in conservatory was before Cervantes."

He was speaking of Ignacio Cervantes, the Cuban composer who died in 1905. A conversation with Valdés tends to go this way: an immersion in a full history of Cuban music, stretching from the days of Spanish rule, to Yoruban *abakuá* chants, to *contradanzas* to mambo to modern Latin jazz. At the mention of Cervantes's name, he sat at the piano and performed all of Cervantes's short "Danza No. 1."

"One of Cervantes's parents was German, and he was sent to Germany to study," he said, on a tangent. "*Entonces,* he was Lecuona's favorite. You can't criticize Cervantes. He did wonderful things, but rhythmically, he copied Saumell." (This reference was to Manuel Saumell Robredo, considered the father of Cuban *contradanza*.)

He played part of "Danza No. 1" again, emphasizing the five-note pattern called the *cinquillo*. "The *cinquillo* was present in the *contradanza*," he explained, "and then Saumell Cubanized it, with Cuban melody and rhythm in the *cinquillo*. The blacks from the Antilles were the ones who took that rhythm to New Orleans. There are rhythms I've heard played at New Orleans funerals that I recall from the *cabildos*," the African neighborhood associations in Cuba.

He got back to Lecuona. "You know who he reminds me of?

My Chucho. He was a child prodigy, and he could really play from the age of four. There are passages there where he was playing bitonally—in two different tones—and I didn't know that could be done at the time," he said. "Really, he's doing three things at the same time. The left hand plays the accompaniment, and the right hand the melody. On top of that, there's a lot of improvising."

Valdés appreciates difficulty. "He had a great left hand, and he wrote for it," he said, returning to his piano and trying to play one of the lines in the music. "There are a lot of tenths in the music." Valdés demonstrated, but suddenly he wasn't playing Lecuona anymore; he was playing a boogie-woogie bass line with his left hand. "It's very difficult to play boogie-woogie, too."

Lecuona, he explained, developed his prodigious talents early, performing in public from the age of nine. "He was a great person, Ernesto, and a great musician. He had lots of women singing for him, students, and they all cooked for him, too. When he won a piano competition in Paris, in 1928, they asked him to play something of his own, and he played 'La Comparsa.'" (It has become one of Cuba's most famous songs.) "The ovation was enormous. With the money he made from winning the competition, he bought himself a farm which he called 'La Comparsa.'"

Valdés started reminiscing again. "A man told me once that Lecuona could be the world's greatest pianist when he was in good spirits, but when he was in a bad mood, or had some kind of problem, he could be the absolute worst."

Was it just his mood—not drinking, or anything like that?

"Oh, no, he didn't drink," Valdés said, waving a big hand. "Just coffee. He smoked a lot of cigarettes, and his fingers were all yellow from nicotine. But he didn't eat much, and he was asthmatic.

"I think maybe it's spiritual," he mused. "When we were filming *Calle 54*, I didn't know what to play. So I played 'La Comparsa,' and a lot of people say it's their favorite tune in the movie."

We moved on to Art Tatum. "My favorite pianist!" he boomed. "He and Bill Evans." He played Evans's "Waltz for Debby," complete with a full chorus of rigorous improvisation. "I love to improvise," he said.

Turning back to Tatum, we listened to "Without a Song," Tatum solo, from the 1955 recordings made at a private party in Beverly Hills. It is rhapsodic, with tremendous, crashing, full-keyboard runs—always through appropriate chord changes—functioning as stepping-stones. "It's virtuosic in technique—totally classical, with modern harmony," he said. "He was the first pianist I ever heard playing modern harmonies and playing them with *heart*. The runs he plays without ever making a mistake—and on top of that, he was blind! The first pianist I ever listened to in American music was Eddy Duchin," he noted, picking out a little bit of "Heart and Soul." "But when I heard Tatum, he wiped out everyone."

Tatum had a kind of orchestral idea for the piano, I suggested. He was everything at once. Valdés disagreed. He understands the word *orchestral* to mean sealed off to improvisation. "But he never played rhythmically," he said, meaning he never played in straight, fixed rhythm. "He was always improvising. He would change time signatures, put one harmony on top of another. I try to imitate him at times, but who am I?"

In the 1940s, Valdés wrote a piece called "Oleaje." It was included on *Bebo Rides Again*, his comeback album; it is also near the end of *Bebo*, his carefully pedagogical solo record of songs by Cuban composers that covers nearly two hundred years. He wrote it thinking of Tatum and his wide, arpeggiated flourishes.

I don't think Tatum ever made it to Cuba, I said. "No," he said. "I also know that he died in 1956." (He was right.) Yet Valdés heard lots of Tatum records in Cuba. "There was a constant flow from America to Cuba," he explained. "Americans used to buy summer homes and retirement homes in Cuba. Sinatra and all those guys used to go there all the time. A lot of the places I played were American owned—mafia or no mafia. It was almost like a colony."

When Valdés was solidifying his reputation in Cuba, several compatriot musicians were reorienting jazz in New York City. (He never spent time there; the only possible American visa available to him was for twenty-nine days, and he wasn't interested in such a short stay.) Mario Bauzá, who had left Cuba in 1930, became enormously influential to Dizzy Gillespie. In 1947, Gillespie's big band was joined by Chano Pozo, who drilled the band in how to play Cuban grooves, particularly the *tumbao,* the repeated bass pattern. (It was a new combination for everyone; even in Cuba, big bands were only beginning to use congas.) The great document of this period is the song "Manteca," a hit record for Gillespie.

Valdés believes that Gillespie's American band played the Cuban rhythms perfectly. He put the track on. "I really hear the conga and the changes in the bass. And the part going *boom-BAH, boom-BAH*"—he imitated the baritone saxophone—"that's all the *tumbao* of mambo," he said. "It's completely the mambo style of Cachao." The song lifted out of Cuban rhythm and into swing, with more arranged harmony, and he savored the shift. "Yeah!" he yelled, enjoying the swing rhythm just as much.

Right after this, he put on a Frank Sinatra record from 1960, "Nice 'n' Easy," arranged by Nelson Riddle. It has the easy midtempo bounce of Sinatra records at the time, and this thrilled Valdés. "Nobody can play music like that except in America, that kind of swing, that time," he said. "It's impeccable. The most difficult thing in the world is to play slowly and keep time. When I listen to this, I see American black people dancing."

Was Sinatra known to listen to Cuban bands a lot?

"Yes," he said, with certainty.

So what's the secret Cuban influence in a record like this?

"I think it's really an Italian influence," he said, laughing. "No, it's just that a lot of things that are called American really come from the Antilles. Like his incredible sense of swing. Yet America, from the thirties to the fifties, gave a lot of music to the world, of which we are all the children. Even though I'm Cuban, I'm really an American arranger," he reflected. "Because the way I write has as much to do with American music as it does with Cuban music. And at the same time it has to do with the fugue." (An example of his fugue writing comes in the middle of "Devoción," part of his "Suite Cubana.")

Chediak pointed out that fugues have little to do with Cuban or American music. "Yes, but I do it anyway," said Valdés. "Why shouldn't I, if I know how?"

We broke for lunch. Valdés puttered around nonstop in the kitchen, bringing out ham and tomato sandwiches, coffee, fruit. He refused to sit down. When we were finished, he brought out the sheet music to Rachmaninoff's Piano Concerto no. 2 in C Minor, to use as a reference as we listened to it.

"I was studying composition and harmony when I heard this performed by the Havana Symphony, in the forties," he said.

What he wanted to show was how the composer can build up a beautiful, fragile melody, then protect it as the orchestra swells around it. "When I hear the music build to a crescendo, I feel like crying," he said.

I asked whether he was able to use this device in his own arranging. "Whenever I can get away with it!" he said. He put on the *guajira* section of the "Suite Cubana," called "Copla no. 4," to demonstrate. It has the same effect: big, brass-heavy crescendos, building in intensifying shades and colors around the melody.

"When you know classical music, you can do what you want to do," he said, and then recited an old maxim to indicate that he had succeeded on his own terms: "*Es mejor ser la cabeza de un perro que la cola de un tiburón.*" It's better to be the head of a dog than the tail of a shark.

Set List

Ernesto Lecuona, "La Paloma," from *The Ultimate Collection—Lecuona* (RCA), recorded 1928.

Art Tatum, "Without a Song," from *20th Century Piano Genius* (Verve), recorded 1955.

Dizzy Gillespie, "Manteca," from *Dizzy Gillespie: The Complete RCA Victor Recordings: 1937–1949* (RCA), recorded 1947.

Frank Sinatra, "Nice 'n' Easy," from *Nice 'n' Easy* (Capitol), recorded 1960.

Sergei Rachmaninoff, Piano Concerto no. 2 in C Minor, *Rhapsody on a Theme of Paganini*, Vladimir Ashkenazy, piano; London Symphony Orchestra, conducted by André Previn (Universal/Penguin Classics), released 1990.

9

It's Your Spirit

Dianne Reeves

"It's been cold here lately," Dianne Reeves said, readying plates of food for a late lunch at her house, "so I decided to make some lamb."

She laid out the meal on the center island of her kitchen, including sweet iced tea made from hibiscus leaves brought home from Turkey and cornbread that she had been perfecting, trying to replicate a version she admired at a local restaurant in Denver. Explaining how she likes to cook, she said: "It's the same thing with how I sing. I work with my ear and try to make it feel right, or I just keep changing it until I like the way it tastes."

So does every musician. But from Reeves this formula sounds excessively humble. She isn't stumbling around in the dark; she has the training, the tools, the instrument. Hers is a big and forthright voice, one that sounds as if it might have been trained over the blare of a touring big band, except that such a model hardly exists anymore.

She is a jazz singer who has absorbed some of the loftiest and most difficult models: Sarah Vaughan, Betty Carter, Shirley Horn.

She treats standards with skyscraper authority, drawing a circle of repertory wide enough to include material from her favorite singer-songwriters; she has her own vocal and performance devices, subdividing vowels into a dozen notes, pouring forth welcomes and singsong advice to her audience.

In 2005, she recorded songs for the soundtrack of the film *Good Night, and Good Luck*, and climbed into the sound-world of the 1950s without contrivances; she won her fourth Grammy for it. In the film she played the role of a nameless singer performing in a warren of broadcast studios down the hall from Edward R. Murrow; she sang the standards with a small backing group, a setup reasonably close to the trio she has used since 2003.

There exists a set of listeners who would hear Reeves rather than any other jazz singer alive sing a standard like "Embraceable You," because she can do so much to it, so imperiously, without soaking it in affectation and becoming ingratiating. Singing other people's songs, Reeves delivers a mixture of might and reserve.

On the other hand, she is better known for her own songs, which reflect more of her own character and opinion, and are often concerned with, as she puts it, "telling stories"; they are miniature studies about hope and memory and keeping despair at bay. They hit a lightly counseling, *Essence* magazine chord, encouraging pride and self-reliance.

She has been a long time forming. The present version of Dianne Reeves comes after thirty years of wending among swing-based jazz, West Coast pop-jazz of the 1980s, and versions of black-diaspora songs and bossa nova from jobs with Harry Belafonte and Sergio Mendes. And before that, a lot of church singing.

Yet Reeves seems firmly of a place and time: the middle of

America and the middle of the twentieth century. This comes out in her manners but also in her preoccupation with spirituality, and with a protective psychology that can accommodate frailty and self-doubt.

As we talked about music and performance, she mentioned several times—to my surprise—the fear and intimidation she feels on stage. I sensed that we were on the verge of a larger conversation, but it was not forthcoming. Later I recognized that same revealing-and-obscuring in one of her more popular songs, "The First Five Chapters." It is a talked-sung narrative about overcoming (a very Dianne Reeves word) a life's pattern of falling into holes, but never specifies what, exactly, the holes are. Finally, it becomes a grid of questions for the audience to apply to itself.

In the fall of 2006, Reeves turned fifty. Since 1991, she has lived on a well-tended stretch of an arterial parkway in the Park Hill neighborhood of Denver, five minutes from her mother—who lives in the house Reeves grew up in—and not too much farther from her sister. When I visited her, in early 2007, she was home only for a brief stop between tours, but as friends and relatives came in and out of the kitchen through the afternoon, she seemed rooted.

Born in Detroit, she moved to Denver with her mother and her sister at the age of two, after the death of her father. Her grandmother Denverada Howard was born in Denver in 1896. (She was named after the city.) Her grandmother's father was a founding member of Denver's oldest black church, Shorter Community A.M.E. church in East Denver. Reeves belonged to that church but also went to Roman Catholic school with daily mass and attended a Baptist church on Sunday. "For us as kids," she said, "we had the feeling that there was nothing we couldn't do or deal with, because we believed in God and we believed that God would make a way.

"In a lot of ways," she elaborated, "music really saved my life. It really helped me to focus. The stage became a very sacred place, because that was where I had this amazing connection with something higher than myself, where I could create and be out on the edge and be totally comfortable with that edge, creating and feeling and hearing and not thinking, not being inhibited or intimidated."

A test of her belief came during the first school busing experiments in Denver, when Reeves was sent far into South Denver to a white junior high school. It was a tense period; parents of the white children wanted the black children out, and there were racist editorials in the local paper. In retaliation the school's black, Texan music teacher organized a revue that combined the poetry of Langston Hughes and songs like "Blowin' in the Wind," "He Ain't Heavy, He's My Brother," and "Joy, Joy" by the Edwin Hawkins Singers.

"It was a powerful thing, and it served to bring people together," she said. "It really changed my life. I really understood that I wanted to sing songs that meant something to me."

Reeves cleared away the lunch plates and brought two iPods with their speaker-dock to the kitchen table. She had put together a list of music that surprised me on two counts: it didn't include Sarah Vaughan, and it was at least as much about written words as it was about vocal performance.

She decided first to listen to Aretha Franklin. *Amazing Grace*, Franklin's live gospel album, released in 1972, was a record that hit Reeves hard in high school; at the time she was singing Franklin hits with a group of friends who called themselves the Mellow Moods.

"Every time one of her new songs came out, you'd learn it," she said. "But when this came out, it was, like, *ahhh*. By that time, James Brown was talking about 'Say It Loud, I'm Black and I'm Proud,' and on the album cover, she had her hair all tied up, and she had African attire on, sitting in front of the church. It was just *powerful*."

On "Mary Don't You Weep," Franklin at first sounds serene — "We're going to review the story of the two sisters, Mary and Martha," she begins — and then the choir starts applying pressure over a slow tempo, making its refrain eerily quiet, occasionally bursting out to high volume.

"Listen to the backgrounds," Reeves said, and she started banging her hand on the table to the one-*two-three* of the chorus's clapping. Franklin enters into a complex series of actions with the band and the choir, half rehearsed, half spontaneous. She invokes Lazarus three times; the third time she hollers, and the choir goes off like a siren. "Woo!" Reeves answered it.

"It's the spirit," she decided. "It's what she knew about, what she learned growing up as a child in her father's church. For the people in the congregation it's a statement of faith and belief. But it's also that whole thing of 'Let's gather around, and I'm going to tell you this amazing story.' I grew up with people telling stories like that, especially after big dinners. It would start here" — Reeves put both hands together down on the table — "and as they go on and go on, and as you become part of the story, it became bigger and bigger." She spread her arms apart.

"A lot of times, there's certain things she says — like, when she talks about Lazarus, when she says his name — I don't think that was ever rehearsed, that part," she said. "It's just call and response, because at that point, everybody is connected, everybody's involved.

They know the Good News of the story; they want to celebrate this story; this is why they're here. And then she has this amazing ability, with her voice, to bring the story that everybody's heard many, many times, and do it in a way that just wears people out. It's like a frenzy. I'm *sure* that after that, they had to get everybody back to normal and cool. I'm sure they had to edit out all of those things. When I listen to it now, it still gets to me. I can't imagine what it was like to actually be there."

When she heard this, I asked, did she want to be this kind of a singer? "Not that kind of a singer; I wanted to have that kind of *spirit*," she corrected. "You know, people always talk about 'what is jazz,' and it's really hard to describe. But one thing I do know is that it's a very intimate exchange between everyone on stage, giving inspiration and ideas to each other; and the other part that's magical for me is when the audience is in on it.

"When they come in and really get it—when they're an active, listening audience—it's like, note one, they have it, they're on board," Reeves continued. "And any subtle thing you do, they'll get it. Aretha says the word *Lazarus* three times, and the third time she waits a little, and then she lets out with 'Laz . . .' and people just go crazy. I've seen a lot of artists do this. One person who always moves me is Ahmad Jamal, because he has this ability to bring you to a place and then explode. All of the ones we'll hear today have that special thing: tell that story through words and music, and through silence and waiting and timing."

This is gospel music straight up and down. But, I ask, does listening to Aretha Franklin's phrasing and pacing give her lessons that she applies to, say, "How High the Moon"?

"Oh, absolutely," she said. "It's timing. It's that thing that just makes your spirit rise—that ability to really savor words and savor a story."

Reeves likes talking about music that isn't specific to one generation. "The majority of the stuff I listened to, my parents listened to—until I started listening to Parliament-Funkadelic," she said.

She next chose a track from the 1964 recording *Sam Cooke at the Copa*, another taste she shared with her mother and stepfather. It was the medley of "Try a Little Tenderness," "(I Love You) for Sentimental Reasons," and "You Send Me," and it contains as much vamping as song playing. As with the Aretha Franklin record, Cooke talk-sings his audience through transitions. This was a trick Reeves learned early on, as a performer in high school, especially with her uncle, a bassist with the Denver Symphony who played jazz at his Unitarian church, and in club dates with the pianist Gene Harris, who moved to Denver when she was a high school junior. She hated the spaces between songs, and she needed to figure out what to do about them.

At first Cooke sounds as if he's stalling: "Oh I never, never/I never, never, never, never, never treat you wrong darling," he sings, adding on a wordless falsetto figure that Ronald Isley would later borrow and turn into his own trademark.

Cooke framed these vamps as metasongs. He's singing to the men in the audience, he declares, because men "have a tendency to neglect the ladies." And as he sings he puts the lyrics in quotation marks, recasting them as mollifying speeches men can deliver to their women. He improvises through the vamping, and he cues the band when he's ready to enter the song. "And also, you have to tell her, 'Darling, you send me,'" he sings, conversationally. "'I wouldn't tell you if I didn't mean it'—that works," he jokes. "'You thrill me, honest you do.'"

Why is that performance such an ideal for her? This record isn't the connoisseur's Sam Cooke, like *Live at the Harlem Square Club* or *Night Beat.* It could be considered Cooke just doing hard-sell business, running through teasers of hits on the way to a surer set-piece. "Because he's standing right on the edge," she answered. "He's thinking; he's forming the words in his mouth. I can tell, because I've been there."

There were other reasons too. "He's so classy. Yeah, that whole idea was you go out onstage and you entertain. You don't bring that other craziness. You bring your joy, and you tell them stories.

"And he's communicating to the band vocally when to start each song," she added. We went back to a few moments just before the band begins "Try a Little Tenderness." "He just cued them," she said, then pointed out another critical moment, just before "You Send Me," where some flutes create a kind of path to the song's entry.

How do we know that in some cases the band isn't cueing him? "Well, in that last case—maybe, I don't know," she said. "You'd have to see it. But that's all part of gospel singing, cueing. And I really think he was in control."

We listened to a song that had nothing to do with jazz or the gospel tradition, "Closer and Closer Apart," by the pop-folk singer Mary Chapin Carpenter. It is a ballad of middle-aged wisdom, about negotiating loss and moral gray areas, about learning to live in a relationship knowing that some of its problems are unsolvable—Keats's ideal of "negative capability" in a love song. Carpenter sings: "[And now] all the king's horses and all the king's men/Wait for their clarion call/Pride hears its voices and fear wins again/And there's nothing to break our fall." ("Mmm," said Reeves, after that line.) "All I can do, is turn now to you/Holding my hand to my heart/All that I know is I'm watching us grow/Closer and closer apart."

"I really understand that song," Reeves said. "All she's doing is expressing a realization of something, but when she says the words, it's like 'Wow, whoa, yes: I know exactly what you're saying. I felt it, but I'd never been able to exactly articulate it.' The thing about *what we always fall back into is our fear*? That's so real."

Did she mean that the song helped her recognize her own patterns in herself? "Yeah," she said. "Beautifully. It also shows you how fragile you are. And also, being able to say, 'I keep going back to you, and I know it's ending, and all I can do is just hold my heart, because I don't want it to end.' So, you can say, 'I want this to end,' but who articulates it like *that*?" She pointed to the iPod. "So, I love her lyrics. If you sing words like that, that's all that's necessary. Where other singers show you what they mean in spaces and silences and colors of notes, she says it in the lyric."

I asked Reeves if she thought women singer-songwriters had a particular aptitude for that kind of writing. "Oh, yeah," she said quickly. "There was a Joan Armatrading song called 'If Women Ruled the World': "No more wars/no more hate/women can fight but talking's great/behind your back or to your face/they'd rather talk than murder.'" She paused. "I always think about that lyric. I might talk about you and call you everything but a child of God, but I don't want you to die. We have this ability to be in touch with certain kinds of feelings, and a lot of these things come from our nurturing spirit. That's what I hear in this music—our spirit that wants to put everything on the table and say, 'If we can find a solution, or if we can't, may God continue to bless you.'"

We continued in this fragile, melancholic direction. Reeves had been eager to talk about a solo-piano piece by Brad Mehldau that she loved called "Memory's Tricks," from the album *Elegiac Cycle.* It's a little more than nine minutes long and goes through several stages. It rapidly runs past its sorrowful introduction, warming into a fast, wakeful rhythm, building contrapuntal waves out of baroque staccato phrases, with tumbling, stormy improvisations. Then it ends in a completely different place, more minimal and pecking. It's classical music, basically, but a kind that could perhaps be invented only by a jazz musician.

"It starts out real distorted, but trying to be beautiful," Reeves explained. "I listened to this and thought, 'Gosh, I have had weeks and days with a feeling exactly like this music sounds'—as you're changing from season to season in your life, as you continuously try to make sense of a lot of things. I'm always trying to look at myself and say, 'Did I do something to cause this situation? Did I benefit from this situation?' But at the end of the day, I did the best with what I had to work with at the time, and here I am, right now."

"*Elegiac*—I guess that's like 'death,'" she continued. "I feel there are many deaths we experience in our lives, or even in a week. This is a record of new beginnings, more than something sad and mournful."

As she talked about this idea of changes in the course of life, of parts of you that close down and parts that start anew, she seemed to be considering both her personal and her musical choices. "I'm fifty now, and through these last ten years I found that a lot of the things I thought I believed in, when I came to a certain consciousness about them, I realized: this isn't working for me. Going through life, trying to make yourself a better person, listening more clearly, being more conscious, you find certain things falling away because you know better. That's what a lot of this record sounds like to me.

"It's not a record that I put on and sit in the kitchen and cook to," she said. "When we have very rainy days I like to listen to strange things, but they make me feel good. It's almost like, tomorrow, the sun's going to shine. When I listen to this, it doesn't make me feel sad; it just makes me aware."

What else have you listened to on rainy days? I asked.

"There's this album that came out long ago by Nana Vasconcelos called *Storytelling*. I used to listen to it while walking through airports. You have the feeling of being a stranger; it's the sounds of the Amazon, and he's creating it with his voices and sounds and textures and all that. I listen to it for sound. One of the things I know about me as a singer is that I really, really respond to sound, and it could just be someone's harmonic vocabulary; I could sit down and sing with just about anybody."

On the outside, Reeves would seem to have little in common with Shirley Horn, who loved slow tempos and nearly whispered her songs. She chose to listen to "Here's to Life," from Horn's 1992 record of the same name. Horn was a passionate singer, but tough and concise, with a kind of Bogart sibilance. She played piano as well, using those harmonies as an extension of her voice. It is Horn's grip on every fraction of a phrase, and the shadings of emotion she put on the words, that Reeves is drawn to.

She came to Horn's music late and never got to know Horn herself. But by the 1990s, she would see her perform at every possible opportunity. "Growing up, I had this really broad range," she said. I could do *this*"—she sings the word in a very high pitch—"and I could do *that*"—several octaves lower. "When I first started working with Harry Belafonte, we were doing traditional songs from different countries—world music—and I was, like they say, 'smellin' myself.' I thought I had been to the mountaintop and heard everything, and the more complex it was, the more I wanted to sing it. So here was this music and it was very simple, not that many chord changes, but the rhythms would be very complex. As we rehearsed them, I started to understand what the words were about: the song of the Zambezi River and all these things. And when I was able to *see* them, I wanted people to see them like I saw them. That was when words really started to be something to me. I wanted to create stories and show their power."

As we listened, Reeves copied the tiniest details of Horn's vocal performance: the little "mm" added to the end of the line "so give it all you got" in the first verse; the tiny, sharp intake of breath after the line "and all that's good get better," toward the end.

"If you broke it down, you could say it was her phrasing," Reeves said. "But it's beyond phrasing; it's breathing life into an inanimate object. The first time she says, 'Here's to love,' she pulls back. She makes it very tender and simple. The second time she says, 'Here's to love,' the 'love' is bigger. She has this picture into something. Shirley does that. Nina Simone does that. Carmen

McRae does that. If they say *love* in a certain way, they can mean it sarcastically, or like they're passionately in love with you, and you'll understand it.

"On 'Wild Is the Wind,' she says things like, 'Oh my darling, *cling* to me.' It just wears me out. I will play it over and over, and hear the passion. That's in every song she does, whether it's up-tempo or slow. She makes the story feel like something you've experienced, like you're a Peeping Tom.

"When you listen to her, you start to understand what the voice is," she continued. "When I'm working with students, I ask them: putting 'great voice' at the bottom of the list, what do you think makes a great singer? It's obvious with her, and with Aretha, that it's your spirit."

Set List

Aretha Franklin, "Mary Don't You Weep," from *Amazing Grace* (Columbia), recorded 1972.

Sam Cooke, "Try a Little Tenderness"/"(I Love You) for Sentimental Reasons"/"You Send Me," from *Sam Cooke at the Copa* (ABCKO), recorded 1964.

Mary Chapin Carpenter, "Closer and Closer Apart," from *The Calling* (Zoe), recorded 2006.

Brad Mehldau, "Memory's Tricks," from *Elegiac Cycle* (Warner Brothers), recorded 1999.

Shirley Horn, "Here's to Life," from *Here's to Life* (Verve), recorded 1992.

10

This Is My Point

Joshua Redman

The saxophonist Joshua Redman has been one of the most visible jazz musicians of the last fifteen years, and that says something not just about his natural flow as an improviser and his command as a bandleader but about his willingness to use words. Being given the chance to represent jazz to the outside world involves a certain amount of rhetoric, and Redman has been rhetorical, in a friendly, nearly guileless way.

At least since 1996, when he released *Freedom in the Groove*, Redman has been working on a theory of how jazz can share a space with pop. It has to do with sincerity as much as form: acknowledging what musicians truly listen to as they grow up and develop, as much as figuring out a way to make jazz phrasing fit over backbeats. Ultimately, he is playing what he likes and trying to make jazz records that in a gingerly way reflect advances in pop.

"Art, in the world of honest emotional experience, is never about absolutes, or favorites, or hierarchies, or number ones," he wrote in the liner notes to *Freedom in the Groove*. "These days, I listen to, love, and am inspired by all forms of music . . . I feel in much of nineties hip-hop a bounce, a vitality, and a rhythmic infectiousness which I have always felt in the bebop of the forties and fifties. I hear in some of today's alternative music a rawness, an edge, and a haunting insistence which echoes the intense modalism and stinging iconoclasm of the sixties avant-garde."

He has played what he wrote, veering back and forth between mainstream jazz and different versions of funk and pop; for a while he kept a trio rightly called the Elastic Band. Yet he also avoided combative language in that defining statement and in his playing too. He is a well-articulated moderate. Nothing he has said or played has come back to haunt him as either too radical or too traditional.

Lean, shaven-headed, and energetic, Redman speaks with fidgety, amiable confidence, saying "yes" regularly as you make your points, even if he goes on to disagree. He is direct. He wants to engage you, and his music has a kind of uprightness about it, a responsibility, even as it is geared toward pleasure and inclusion.

His father was the great saxophonist Dewey Redman, a poetic improviser, a genius of blues tonality and free improvisation, and an important collaborator with Ornette Coleman and Keith Jarrett. (Dewey Redman died in 2006, just after the birth of Joshua's son, Jadon.) He was raised in Berkeley, California, by his mother, Renee Shedroff, a retired dancer and librarian. In the early years of the new century, he left New York, returning to Berkeley and then Oakland.

I talked with him in 2004, when he was still working as the artistic director of SF Jazz, which organizes a year-round schedule of concerts as well as a jazz festival, and which started its own in-house band, the SF Jazz Collective, with Redman as figurehead. (It was a facile comparison, but one almost had to make it: as the public face of a major jazz institution, Redman was briefly the West Coast version of Wynton Marsalis.) He left the organization and the band in 2006 to make time for his family, but his sense of pluralism had already helped define SF Jazz's program, centering on jazz as it has sounded since the 1950s, and reaching into every other kind of music with which it shares affinities.

Preparing for our conversation, Redman came up with two different lists—a long one and a short one—and nearly thirty records, including Meshell Ndegeocello, Tortoise, Led Zeppelin, D'Angelo, Keith Jarrett, Dexter Gordon, and Björk. It was pretty easy to condense them. For Redman, all other interests recede when you bring up Sonny Rollins and John Coltrane.

One other choice muscled in, a still-current band that many younger musicians see as a creative ideal in jazz: the Paul Motian–Joe Lovano–Bill Frisell trio. We met on a Saturday afternoon in the New York City office of Bob Hurwitz, the head of Redman's record label, Nonesuch. I brought everything with me, but it wasn't necessary; Redman had all the tracks on his traveling laptop and had burned copies of everything.

Rollins is the living exemplar of narrative structure in jazz improvisation, and that is principally what Redman has absorbed from him: the logical, symmetrical, advancing-and-recapitulating, storytelling impulse. We listened to "St. Thomas," the calypso track from Rollins's 1956 album *Saxophone Colossus*.

"It's funny," Redman said as the track started. "I actually haven't listened to this album for many years. But I went through a period where this was literally the only thing I listened to. I discovered it shortly after I started playing the saxophone, when I was ten. I'd certainly listened to a lot of jazz records—a lot of Coltrane, some Miles, Cannonball Adderley, Ornette Coleman, Keith Jarrett, you know, the musicians who my father was associated with.

"My mom couldn't afford to buy me that many records," he continued, "so I went to the public library in Berkeley, checked this out, came home, put it on, and here was the first track. And it was, for me, as monumental an experience as I've had listening to music. It unlocked a door to the potential of what improvisation really could be."

I asked if it was as if he hadn't realized before that one could do that sort of thing out loud.

"Exactly," Redman answered, sharply. "Exactly. I certainly was very familiar and comfortable with the idea of improvisation—I mean, the way I started playing music was by improvising. I never really had any formal musical lessons. But what Sonny showed me was that you could be completely spontaneous and at the same time have this unerring sense of logic and structure." He paused briefly. "He shows you how effortlessly the two can be fused. You don't ever get the sense that he's sitting back, outside of himself, thinking about the architecture from a kind of third-party view. You don't ever get the sense that he's playing licks, even when he plays something that you know he's played before. It never sounds like, two-five, lick, insert." (Here Redman was talking about the ii-V changes, the most basic harmonic progression in jazz.)

After the opening theme statement, Rollins plays a two-note pattern, messes around with it, and comes back to it again. "As symmetrical as it is," said Redman, struck by it anew, "it still has the element of surprise. It's not bland; it's not derivative. And he's going to do it again here." The same two notes, the fifth and first degrees of the scale, return to close the next chorus. "It's like you couldn't have written it better, but you couldn't have written it. You know?"

This has been the overriding view of Rollins since Gunther Schuller wrote "Sonny Rollins and the Challenge of Thematic Improvisation," a persuasive essay published in the *Jazz Review* in November 1958. But Redman's deeper point is that Rollins heightens your awareness to what really *is* possible. "He makes it sound easy. And yes, he makes you think you can do it, and he makes you really *want* to do it." He stopped cold to hear Rollins play a singsong five-note line and then repeat it eight more times, just before Tommy Flanagan's piano solo.

"There's a quality about Sonny Rollins's playing that makes improvisation acceptable. No, it isn't easy," he said, smiling. "You do have to immerse yourself in the language. And the more you try to do it like him, the more you realize how freakin' hard it is."

We listened to it again, picking out a few strange points. One occurs in Rollins's second solo, after Max Roach's drum break, when Rollins plays three braying, stubborn, bending notes that unravel the eighth-note swing he's established. I suggested that he's doing a few different things here: asserting control and elbowing the listener, as if to ask, "Are you still with me?"

"It's definitely assertive," Redman agreed. "I don't know how much I feel it's like asking the listener that. It's very different from the way Illinois Jacquet would use repetition in his 'Jazz at the Philharmonic' solos—you know, riff-based repetition to get the band going and get the crowd going. That's very powerful and exciting, but it's a kind of specific device. To me, Sonny's use of repetition is not like that. It's always in service of a flow. It's as if he were speaking to you and he made a point, and he makes that point again, and again. It's just like, '*This is my point*, and now I'm moving on.'"

Another point arrived at the start of the bridge of the following chorus: "Ohhh . . . ," Rollins interjects, before generating the next new phrase. "He's going for something," Redman said. "He's got this idea, and maybe it didn't come out, or the idea is just a second before the execution, so he's like 'ohhh!' Then he plays. It reinforces the fact that this is so off-the-cuff. He's out there in the wilderness, like we all are when we're trying to improvise."

Redman is an on-the-one-hand, on-the-other kind of talker and by extension tacks naturally toward self-effacing comments, often to the effect that he hasn't heard enough, or that he can never reach the level of understanding or sheer musicianship of someone else. "Listening to an improvisation like this," he continued, "I'm struck by the mastery and the seriousness of it, as this perfectly constructed, spontaneous narrative. And at the same time, there's this quality in Sonny: he cautions you against taking anything too seriously."

Redman knew he wanted to talk about Coltrane, but thought it might be too obvious, and then fretted about what to choose. Since he felt the album suite *A Love Supreme* was too sacred to pick apart, he chose *Transition*, from 1965, one of the last recordings of the intact Coltrane quartet, with the pianist McCoy Tyner, the bassist Jimmy Garrison, and the drummer Elvin Jones. "It's pretty long, so let's just play it and start talking. It's going to be a little sacrilegious for me," he confessed, "but hey."

Transition isn't an album often cited as anyone's favorite. In the time line of Coltrane's career, it sits just inside the period when he started to make individual pieces that sounded rather alike, often built on a single mode. What does Redman hear in it? "The sheer force of it," he replied, quickly. "As far as a single piece of Coltrane with the classic quartet, it has perhaps the greatest force, impact, feeling of surrender, you know, abandon, devotion. I had been listening to Coltrane since the day I was born, probably, but someone turned me on to this record in college."

After Berkeley High School, Redman went to Harvard in 1987, eventually completing a premed degree while edging closer to jazz and playing with musicians from Boston's Berklee College of Music in the summertime. "Someone from Berklee hipped me to this," he recalled. "I think it might have been Mark Turner, I don't quite remember, but someone said, 'Man, if you think the other stuff is potent, check this out.' I remember thinking, 'How could it get more intense?' " As he was talking, Coltrane had moved up to the next level in his soloing, chipping up his fast and assured middle-register runs with high shrieks on the tenor saxophone.

"With this track, from the beginning, there's no intro, there's no lead-in," he said. "It's just, like, *bam*: here we are at the apex. You can't go any higher. Yet they keep climbing and climbing, and then they come down a little bit, and then they climb again."

He also observed—and liked—that Coltrane, here, was trying to place all his studies in harmony within a freer and more furious style. "If you pay attention to the notes that Trane is playing," Redman said, "you hear the harmonic sophistication of what he's playing, all these complex devices and maps that he's created for himself. You can hear him playing 'Giant Steps' stuff in there," chordal and melodic movement in thirds, which Coltrane had built into that composition six years earlier.

We started the piece over again from the beginning: Jones hits the downbeat, and Coltrane lines out a scale. "You know, that was the melody, basically. It's so simple. And just the quality of Trane's sound," he remarked. "It sounds like he's screaming and praying at the same time. He's playing so much horn, so much technically, so much harmonically; the constituent elements of what he's playing are so complex. Yet it's like he's trying to blow the horn apart and just play his emotions through the instrument."

Redman said he was moved by it spiritually, but then allowed that he wasn't a religious person and hadn't been raised religiously.

What do you mean by *spiritual*? I thought.

At this point, Coltrane returned in the track, going up so high, with so much force, that Redman laughed. He apologized for sounding new agey, then went ahead. "At certain times in my life this music has kind of swept me up and transported me to a place where I can sense that there is something greater than the material existence of things. And a fabric that binds the material world together and offers an escape from that world. This is definitely one of the last for this band where everything is still happening around a tonic center, a mode. It's in D-something: D-Phrygian, D-Dorian. And they're still operating in these even-numbered bar phrases. Not when Coltrane's playing, but the way McCoy and Elvin interact, every sixteen bars, there's that big crash on the cymbal and the bass drum, and McCoy playing the root and the fifth. That was a style that they introduced in '62 or '63, I guess, but here you hear it at its furthest development. You can hear the band pushing the limits of its style. You can hear Trane's desire to escape. Part of Elvin is pushing in that direction too, but part of him wants to stay, wants to keep those cycles in place. McCoy probably even more so than Elvin. You can hear that McCoy is a little bit closer to the ground. And so you can hear a little tension in the group."

It's still mysterious, I said, how Coltrane started going all-out during this period, just as a matter of course. "Yeah," he said, "I can't imagine doing that. But the sense you get from Trane is total commitment. I think that exists for all of us jazz musicians, as this *ideal*. I mean, he's like an ideal type, a Platonic ideal. He represents something I could never be and, I think, most jazz musicians could never be, but that I want to strive for as much as I can."

We had a brief Aristotelian conversation about modes, and what feelings they effect in the listener, but Redman eventually shifted back down to his root position of awe. "It's difficult and dangerous to try to talk about what Coltrane was trying to do, using these different musical elements. Was he consciously saying, 'This drone allows me to create *this*?' I don't get that sense. I don't get the sense that there was that element of being outside of the music, or removed from it. In fact, precisely the opposite: no one else was so inside his music. It's completely first-person."

It is now understood better than ever that great bands, more than great individuals, make jazz matter in the larger culture. "This group," he said, "the Coltrane quartet, has had a profound influence in terms of making us aware of the importance of a group, and that the greatest groups are greater than the sum of their individual parts. This is not music of individuals. This is not the music of John Coltrane and his rhythm section. It's the music of four men under the leadership of John Coltrane, but what's being created here is a true group undertaking. And this is in contrast to the Sonny Rollins track, in which there's that feeling of Sonny being out front, making his statement, and everyone else kind of supporting him. Here, everybody is wholly committed to the cause.

"It's always been very important to me to have a regular working band," he continued. "Right now, this is the first time that I haven't really had one. The Elastic Band has been on hiatus. I've been doing some acoustic trio stuff, too. But not one of them is a full-time, year-round commitment. I think the most interesting jazz these days doesn't take the form of a soloist backed by accompanists; it takes the form of a group interacting, improvising together."

This is a central belief among many musicians of Redman's generation in jazz. He was born in 1968, and his Rosetta stones are bands, not individuals: Coltrane's "classic" quartet; Ornette Coleman's late 1950s and early 1960s quartets; Miles Davis's mid-1960s quintet; Bill Evans's early 1960s trios; and Keith Jarrett's mid-1970s American quartet, with Redman's father, Dewey, on saxophone.

In the mid-1990s, Redman was among the last beneficiaries of major-label largesse in jazz; Warner Brothers helped lodge him into popular culture. He made an appearance on *Arthur*, the children's television show, as a cartoon version of himself. He toured with the Rolling Stones, playing the solo in "Waiting on a Friend," originated by Sonny Rollins. He appeared in fashion magazines. He appeared on talk shows. (A couple, anyway.)

But this is all history; he's a working musician. More recently he has become part of a few other people's bands, too: the guitarist Kurt Rosenwinkel and the keyboardist Sam Yahel. That version of Rosenwinkel's band existed only for several months in 2003; after touring Europe, it recorded *Deep Song,* one of the better places to hear a rawer, more adventurous side of Redman's playing.

He first played with Rosenwinkel at Smalls, the club in New York City's West Village that opened in 1994. Redman was already established by then, having played at the Village Vanguard with his father in 1990, signed to Warner in 1991, and recorded his first album in 1992. "I had subbed for Mark Turner a few times in Kurt's band in the midnineties, at Smalls, and it was always really inspiring," he said. "But I always felt kind of like a sad substitution for Mark Turner." Though he was the one with the much greater fame, it wasn't until he played again with Rosenwinkel in 2003 that he felt comfortable amid that group's fluid collective improvising.

That isn't surprising. Redman isn't as much of a superstitious worrier as his hero Rollins, but he does share certain cautious traits, which tend to come out on his sometimes overdetermined records. It was clear, to anyone who saw him in his early performing years, that he could do remarkable things within a saxophone-bass-drums trio: he had the flow, the freshness, the stamina. But he didn't display it, at least not on record, for fourteen years—not until 2007, on *Back East*, the best record he has ever made.

The record isn't a Sonny Rollins homage per se, yet it explicitly, thunderingly references him—in the use of the saxophone trio, which Rollins first made famous; in its material ("Wagon Wheels," "I'm an Old Cowhand," both from Rollins's *Way Out West* album);

and in the title. But it doesn't matter. Somehow copping to his Rollins obsession freed him. In his trio concerts with Reuben Rogers on bass and Eric Harland on drums that followed the album's release, Redman tore through advanced sequences and patterns with personal authority; he was playing lots of notes but giving all of them meaningful relationships, too.

Talking about the importance of groups brought him to "It Should Have Happened a Long Time Ago," by the Paul Motian–Joe Lovano–Bill Frisell trio, from the 1994 album *Trioism*. "That's the highest level of free group improvisation that you can get," he said, when he first brought up the idea of listening to the track.

"It's kind of like magic," Redman said, as the track started misting out of the speakers, with saxophone, guitar, and drums playing fragile counterlines against one another. "The sense of three musicians becoming one." After the group reached the end of the melody, he continued. "I mean, now they've finished the song, I *guess*, but who's soloing?" Lovano's saxophone extrudes a short line. "Joe's kind of soloing, but Bill's in there. This is true group improvisation, and it's not just melodic improvisation.

"Right there, they're playing in a minor key, and Joe introduces the major third. All of a sudden it's this new color, and Bill picks up on it. It's not like one person is soloing and other people are accompanying. And secondly, it's not like the improvisation is happening in only one realm. It's group improvisation in the melodic realm, in the harmonic realm, in the rhythmic realm."

We went back and listened again to the major third coming in. "It's astounding," he reacted, "the degree to which they're listening and reacting to one another, the sense in which each voice will kind of come to the fore and then recede in a completely continuous way. It's so fluid. It's like water."

Set List

Sonny Rollins, "St. Thomas," from *Saxophone Colossus* (Prestige), recorded 1956.

John Coltrane, "Transition," from *Transition* (Impulse!), recorded 1965.

Paul Motian Trio, "It Should Have Happened a Long Time Ago," from *Trioism* (Winter & Winter), recorded 1994.

11

Labor History

Hank Jones

The last sixty years of jazz seems to be retained in the pianist Hank Jones's head: a labor history of all the jam-session, studio, one-night, and concert-hall gigs he has played since moving to New York City in 1944. Jones has been one of the hardest and most consistent workers in the history of jazz. As a result, his focused, organized, subtle touch—one of his devices is to turn up the energy of his improvising while still playing softly—shows up repeatedly in any accounting of the music.

The recorded history of Jones's playing begins with a Hot Lips Page session in 1944 and then works through Charlie Parker and Billy Eckstine and Artie Shaw and Ella Fitzgerald. It gets a bit obscure in the 1960s—Jones was working as a staff musician at CBS from 1955 to 1972—but becomes fully trackable again in the mid-1970s, with a serious renewal of his trio playing.

Unlike Oscar Peterson, he never had a Norman Granz to keep his career consistent and to control the flow and quality of his recordings. Since the 1970s, his discography has become a bramble; no other jazz musician of his stature has made so many records for so many labels, some of them great, others homely or compromised or badly conceived. Once I saw him play a gig in a senseless trio, set up by a record producer, with Omar Hakim, the loud-and-bland fusion drummer. It was like a Ford Escalade against a loom, or a watchmaker's lathe. I know I'm mixing metaphors; the performance did that, too. But he rolled on unperturbed, retaining his professionalism.

When I got together with Jones in 2005, he was having a stout year: working in Joe Lovano's spectacular quartet, with the bassist George Mraz and the drummer Paul Motian, and getting ready to release a new trio record, *For My Father*, under his own name, at age eighty-seven. After all these years, Jones plays as if hitting the highest level of small-group jazz playing were as easy as walking. He has the sound of wisdom.

Jones rarely listens to jazz at his home in Hartwick, New York, near Cooperstown, where he lives with his wife, Theodosia. When he isn't working, he prefers to practice, two to four hours a day, rather than hear anyone else's music. What's the point of accepting a mediated version of jazz, when you can trace its family tree through your own life and work? (If you had been around Nat King Cole as a fellow musician, as Jones was, and heard him play at his best in jam sessions, Nat King Cole records might sound to you like contrivances.) Anyway, Jones likes to keep his focus on what is to be done tomorrow.

In his gracious way, Jones posed a challenge to my project. He stalled at step one: given the assignment, to which he quickly agreed, he had a Bartleby-like resistance toward choosing any music in particular.

"I'm really not much of a listener," he explained in a preliminary phone conversation. We isolated a few areas of interest, including solo style, small-group arrangement, unaccompanied piano, and pianists backing up singers. Beyond that, he left it up to me.

He had one other desire, though: "I'd like to choose something by Count Basie," he said. "Because everything he did was so unpretentious."

We met at a hotel room in midtown Manhattan one evening, during one of his visits to the city for meetings and rehearsals. His day's work was done, but he greeted me in a coat and tie. Jones spoke rapidly, with a melodious roll in his voice; when forming an opinion, his eyes flashed. Records may not mean much to him per se, but when zeroing in on individual performances, he was an astute, original thinker.

When Jones was a young musician working in Detroit during the late 1930s and early '40s, Art Tatum was important to him, along with Teddy Wilson, Fats Waller, and Earl Hines. "They represented a level I was trying to attain," he said. "Trying to attain. I'm not saying I ever attained that level, but you keep trying. It's a never-ending process."

Talking about his strivings as a pianist, or about his betters, he adopted a different tone. He never lost focus and became resigned or defeated; on the contrary, he grew factual and energized. And Tatum was the one pianist Jones talked about most as a paradigm, though a conceptual one rather than a practical one.

"As far as Tatum is concerned, it may take a few hundred years before I can get there," he said. "I don't want to play exactly like Tatum. I'd like to adapt some of his technical ideas, but as far as imitating him note for note, I don't think that's good for anybody. I've heard pianists who can play Tatum's solos, or at least that's how it sounds. But there's one thing about creativity. You can do that with classical pieces, even the most difficult—you can play them note-for-note, the way the composer wrote them, right? Or you could play Tatum's solos, if you had the technique. But the inventiveness, the creativity, is not there.

"It's one thing to interpret, in other words, and it's another thing to create," he concluded. "Tatum did both simultaneously: creative and interpretive. Simultaneous composition, you might say."

Jones first heard Tatum in the late 1930s, at his family home in Pontiac, Michigan, on a radio broadcast from Detroit. (By 2005, he was the last survivor of ten siblings, who included two other superior musicians: the drummer Elvin Jones and the trumpeter Thad Jones.) Then, he was convinced that the Tatum broadcast was actually two pianists, with the gimmick of sounding like a single, invincible one. Later, after moving east, he finally saw Tatum in Buffalo, where Jones's band was working at the Anchor Bar, and Tatum was at McVan's, across town. Jones watched Tatum each night after work. "Funny thing is, he was playing on a piano which wasn't a grand; it was a spinet," Jones said. "But he made it sound like a Steinway D."

I chose a solo performance of "Sweet Lorraine" from Tatum's 1955 private-party recordings in Los Angeles. Jones had heard the recordings, but it had been a while; though he didn't anticipate the details, he quickly picked up on them, as if they pricked his memory. Before the first bridge, Jones started chuckling; in the bridge, Tatum dislodges a titanic, disruptive run, a microcomposition in itself, referring to the song's chords along the way. Then, for comic effect, he quotes the melody of "Nobody Knows the Trouble I've Seen." Jones laughed again.

"One of the most impressive things is, of course, those runs," he said, "which he played at blinding speed with either hand, and he sort of set up the next chord progression with them. And the run itself is, of course, a chord progression; you can hear the chords in there. A lot of people say, 'Why does he play all those runs?' Well, they're an integral part of his style."

So what a lot of people take as exclamation points, or pure ornament, was really functional for Tatum, a means of binding all the action together? "In a sense they're exclamation points," Jones said. "It's like we're having a conversation, and the runs illustrate where he's going, or maybe illustrate that part of the melodic harmonization or harmonic progression that he's using. Melodic, harmonic; they're interchangeable. They're not separate; they're part of a whole. He integrated everything so well that you can't separate any one part from another.

"But without the runs, what he was doing would probably not be as effective. He made a lot of excursions. He'd spot a progression, and on the way there, he takes a little excursion and plays a run to illustrate his point; maybe he's describing something that he saw on the way there and on the way back," he said. "His playing is very descriptive, you know."

We listened to it again, starting from the beginning. "He

definitely shows you parts of the melody," Jones said, during Tatum's introduction. "Now here he goes," he said, at the obvious beginning of the melody proper. The first real explosion of technique went off during the bridge and startled Jones. "His playing is almost beyond description!" he said.

At the end of one chorus, as it led into the next, Tatum's run set up the harmonic motion to follow. During the longest, most percussive run in the performance, Jones's face lit up. "You see? He's changing chords with every beat of that run."

Another bridge came along, with another excursion. "Everything he does is a concerto," Jones said, wonderingly. "He knows exactly what he's doing."

I asked Jones who else impressed him when he was working in Detroit. "There wasn't a lot of great music being played," he said. "They had a lot of studio bands, radio bands, and there was one guy, Bill Stegmeyer, who later became one of the writers for *The Jackie Gleason Show*, an excellent arranger—he was working with one of those bands. He was an excellent teacher, by the way. I studied with him later." Jones studied classical piano repertory, especially Chopin, with private teachers into his fifties. "And there was a pianist named Lannie Scott, who had a style similar to Art Tatum's. Both Lannie and Art had a trick where they'd play 'Tea for Two' with the left hand and smoke a cigarette with the right."

Jones left Detroit for Cleveland in 1942, working at the Cedar Gardens nightclub, where there were also dancing girls and a comedian. On Sunday afternoons, he said, a fight routinely broke out in the middle of Cedar Street, near the club's front door.

"I think a lot of people came just to see the fight," he noted dryly. "It was very interesting."

Subsequently, he took the gig in Buffalo, where he first saw Tatum, and then moved on to New York City. He deposited his Detroit union card at the New York Musicians' Union, Local 802, and played a series of pickup gigs while waiting the requisite six months before landing an extended job—a rule back then, to limit the bulging union rolls. Then, at the invitation of the saxophonist Lucky Thompson, he joined Hot Lips Page's big band, first at the Onyx Club on Fifty-second Street and then on tour.

"We went out on the road, doing three months of one-nighters," Jones remembered. "And I learned a very valuable lesson at that time. Which was: never do that again."

We pushed on to Count Basie, another of his models. "The thing about Basie, which to me is very significant, is that the band was the main focus," Jones recalled. "He played maybe only an eight-bar or twelve-bar or thirty-two-bar solo. He integrated his style into the big band, which was usually a single-finger style—although I heard him play stride piano, by the way, and he was also a great organist. In a big band you play a lot less, because you have to play in the spots, and that has to relate to the whole. I think he used taste in the best possible way, you know. By not overplaying, and yet being effective. That's very difficult to do—to play minimally and yet have a maximum effect."

We heard "Time Out," from 1937. Jones didn't recall the title but recognized the song after a few seconds. Each player in the

Basie band contributes an equal share to the total sound, with slangy phrasing and a deep, relaxed groove. It's a spacious, natural record. Soloing, Basie starts out with his usual edited phrases, then begins a stride passage and grows more voluble. "Oh?" Jones said at that point, cocking his head and listening hard.

"I heard a certain amount of discipline there," he said, when the song ended. "Duke Ellington had a great band, but it didn't have that kind of discipline, in my estimation. Duke wrote a lot of great music. It's just that when the reed section was playing, you heard a lot of Johnny Hodges, but not a lot of the other horn players."

Starting in 1947, Jones played with Ella Fitzgerald in Norman Granz's Jazz at the Philharmonic concerts. (While many of his colleagues drank or gambled, Jones said, he read novels and practiced the piano.) During this period he developed an admiration for Jimmy Jones—no relation—who became Sarah Vaughan's regular accompanist in the 1950s. (Jones himself didn't work much with Vaughan: only two concerts and a record date.)

He wanted to hear something by that pair, and because he wouldn't put his finger on anything in particular, I chose Vaughan's "Embraceable You," from 1954. It's among the best-known things they did together, but it has a fairly sleepy tempo.

He listened as Jimmy Jones played chords softly, on every beat, under Vaughan. "Jimmy's accompaniment on this particular tune isn't typical of what he could do," he quickly decided. "This is fairly subdued; he's providing a harmonic background, not interfering with her. But I've heard him play accompaniment that, to me, sounded as if he were thinking along the lines of Ravel."

He elaborated a little. "Here he's using what I think of as a continuous style. He's not playing just on fills. He's using a melodic foundation behind her, which is continuous, almost like a counter-melody." Suddenly Jimmy Jones picked out five treble-clef notes, a short, original fill, just before Vaughan sang the line "Come to Mama, do."

"Now, I think Sarah liked those kind of fills," Jones said. "Single-line fills. In my estimation, if you do that, you run the risk of inter-fering with the singer's train of thought. But I think Sarah liked the pianist to lead the train of thought and for her to follow. Ella's pref-erence was for block-chord fills, to make her feel comfortable—never leading, always playing in response to her."

Jones's next request was Charlie Parker, who fit into the same category as Tatum—a virtuosic, fascinating soloist—but whose music also qualifies as great small-band music. (Jones recorded with Bird in the early 1950s.)

I chose "Ah-Leu-Cha," which Jones surprisingly said he didn't recognize, from a 1948 recording. "Perfect control," Jones mut-tered during Bird's first solo, with its clean, strong sound even through double-time runs. "He always had that beautiful tone. And he never played extended solos, maybe two choruses, but that would be all you wanted to hear."

The song banged shut, and Jones laughed again. "Bird would play a thirty-two-bar song, and then he'd play a blues, but he al-ways had that same kind of tone," he said. "That's what makes him distinctive. I think his tone is equally distinctive as his style. They go together. Without the tone, the style wouldn't be as impressive."

What did Parker want from a pianist in his groups? "He required a pianist to follow the chord changes correctly, and not to overplay but just play in spots," Jones said. "Bud Powell did that; Al Haig did it. Anyway, if you didn't listen for a while, you wouldn't know what he was doing. You had to listen to find out what direction he was going in, and you played the fills accordingly.

"Working with Charlie was quite an experience. You always heard something that made you think, and think in the idiom that he was playing in. He'd pull you along with him; you couldn't just play your own way. He'd get you used to the idea of getting outside of yourself, because that's what you have to do."

Jones is one of the few leading musicians left from the early bebop era who can comment on what the greatest players were actually thinking about the new music.

"At that time," he said, "a lot of musicians put that style down. They didn't like it. You'd think that musicians would be the first ones to pick up on it, but a lot of them didn't—'What are these guys *doing*?' I didn't think that at all. My ears were wide open; my brain was receptive. I thought it was a change for the better, harmonically and melodically. It was a very difficult style to learn to play, and it still is. I don't consider myself a master of the style. I consider myself a student of it."

Starting in the late 1950s, Jones had been willing to sacrifice much of what many might consider an artistic life for his steady job doing live radio and television with CBS. He lived then in Cresskill, New Jersey, just across the Hudson River and slightly north of Manhattan, and he couldn't leave the area. "You were always subject to get a call from the contractor for an unexpected rehearsal, so you had to be on the scene," he explained. "It would be four or five, and they'd call and say, 'Can you be here at six o'clock?' This is a.m., mind you."

He worked five days a week and was assigned to a round-robin of variety shows: Ed Sullivan, Jackie Gleason, Garry Moore. He played on two live radio programs—one Dixieland, one modern jazz. He played rehearsals. "I liked the challenge," he said. "Every week there was a different challenge—some kind of sight-reading or adapting to a different style. And of course it was a substantial income; basically it was a year-round job, and it had a pension and health insurance. If you went on the road, you might do well for one tour, but then you might be out of work for six months. Well, that's no good," he said, shaking his head. "Mortgage payments have to be paid."

At this point in our conversation Jones didn't really seem like most of the jazz musicians I know, with their aristocratic pessimism and stubborn aesthetic ideals. Both in his listening and in his bits of autobiography, he reminded me of some other kind of highly refined worker-for-hire: a craftsman with an old-fashioned work ethic, someone sanguine to the truth that he won't be making masterpieces on someone else's clock, but who proudly delivers on time.

I asked if it was even possible, back in the CBS days, to stay up late at jazz clubs. "Well, that's why I had to stop working at the Vanguard," Jones said. (One of the jazz-club jobs he briefly tried to pursue during that time, starting in 1965, was as the pianist with the great, transformative big band led by his brother Thad and the drummer Mel Lewis; they had a regular Monday-night gig at the Village Vanguard.) "They would get out of work at two-thirty, but I had a seven o'clock rehearsal with Jackie Gleason."

"I know I can do better than I'm doing now," he commented, casually, toward the end of our talk.

You really mean that?

"Oh, yeah. There's another level that's reachable. I think it's just a question of time, perhaps, or dedication. I know it's there."

Do you know what it sounds like?

"What you do is imagine what it should sound like," he explained. "Once, I was working on Fifty-second Street with the Coleman Hawkins group. In the group was Max Roach, Miles Davis, and Curley Russell was the bass player." (Jones reckoned this was around 1954. But it must have been 1946 or 1947, when Hawkins, an elder figure, was making a point of playing with the first wave of bebop musicians.) "I was living up on 101st and Madison, and I used to go to work every night on the bus. On this particular night I was a little bit late.

"When I walked in and started playing, I played things that I had not played before. It may have been caused by stress; I don't know what caused it. But I was on a different level at that time. That may sound a little screwball, but that's what happened. You can think thoughts you haven't thought previously.

"I think people like Charlie Parker could do it consciously." He laughed. "I've got to do it subconsciously."

This was steadying to hear. Lateness, mysterious higher levels of accomplishment, the subconscious—now he was sounding very much like a jazz musician.

Set List

Art Tatum, "Sweet Lorraine," from *20th Century Piano Genius* (Verve), recorded 1955.

Count Basie, "Time Out," from *The Complete Decca Recordings* (Verve), recorded 1937.

Sarah Vaughan, "Embraceable You," from *Sarah Vaughan with Clifford Brown* (Polygram), recorded 1954.

Charlie Parker, "Ah-Leu-Cha," from *Best of the Complete Savoy and Dial Studio Recordings* (Savoy Jazz), recorded 1948.

12

Dancing from Up Here

Roy Haynes

On the wall of his wood-paneled basement in suburban Long Island, the drummer Roy Haynes has hung a large poster of his idol, the Count Basie band drummer Jo Jones. In the picture, taken in 1940 in Quincy, Massachusetts, Jones stands outside of a building in a hat, suit, and full-length overcoat, holding a cymbal with his left hand and a brush with his right. The attitude is casual defiance: Jones's feet are spaced apart; his chin and his eyebrows are raised. "He was the man," Haynes said. "And he carried himself like that."

In the summer of 2004 Haynes invited four other drummers to his house in Baldwin, New York, where he lives alone. Haynes, Eddie Locke, Ben Riley, Louis Hayes, and Jackie Williams ended up standing around the picture, drinking champagne and talking about Papa Jo. Likewise, a year later, when I showed up at Haynes's house to talk about music with him, the conversation kept turning back to Jones.

Jonathan Jones, who died in 1985, made the high hat significant in articulating jazz rhythm, and it has ever been thus. He played authoritatively with brushes, not just on ballads. He snapped down his patterns with subtlety and force; he plowed powerful grooves for a band. He didn't get involved in long solos; above all, he had vitality, magnetism. You could learn just by watching him move around. He was confident and inspired some fear. He was proud of his "kiddies," the musicians he influenced. (He became known as Papa Jo in the late 1950s, in part to distinguish him from Philly Joe Jones, Miles Davis's drummer.) Toward the end of his life, he liked to perform sections of concerts on the high hat alone.

Haynes never took a lesson from Jones. But he developed a whole area of technique around the high hat, treating it as an instrument unto itself, building on Jones's principles. Really, he isolates every part of his drum kit in a similar way, letting it sing. He is attention-seeking, breaking up time, making his drum set react, hitting hard, and then leaving space. And he is naturally modern. During our conversation he kept reminding me of his breadth, that his sound must not be too quickly understood, that he plays in many different ways.

But a musician is not only what he plays. Jones approved of Haynes for his self-possession, too. Haynes bought his first car in the summer of 1950, the same week Miles Davis did. "Young jazz musicians buying cars was not heard of," he said, proudly. "Let alone a supposed bebop drummer." When I spent time with Haynes, he was eighty, and he owned four. One was a Bricklin, a rare machine with gull-wing doors, manufactured for only two years in the mid-1970s.

Haynes likes some crackle in his leisure. When he comes into Manhattan and he's not working, he said, he often rents a limousine. "I'm like a little kid. I'm so excited, man. I just party, enjoy." Though he doesn't particularly like gambling, he bought a second house in Las Vegas in 2001; he travels there every few months and goes out to clubs and restaurants with his friends. "I used to play

Vegas when I was with Sarah Vaughan, when there was still preju-
dice. I never thought I'd buy property there."

And the clothes. He often cites his inclusion in a list, created
by *Esquire* magazine in 1960, of the best-dressed men in America.
A musician in his thirties told me he met Haynes one night at the
Village Vanguard. He mentioned to Haynes that he had just played
there himself. "I was wearing jeans and a flannel shirt, and my hair
was dirty," the younger musician recalled. "Roy just looked me up
and down. And then up, and then down again. He said, '*Huh*.'"

Jo Jones was the obvious place to start, and our other subjects
flowed from him. At the top of Haynes's list was Count Basie's
"The World Is Mad," from 1940, with Jones on drums. But since
all CDs that include it have gone out of print, I brought instead a
Basie box set called *America's #1 Band!* since it covers that same period of the band.

We listened to "Swing, Brother, Swing," which is about as good as
American music gets. It comes from a radio broadcast in June 1937,
recorded at New York's Savoy Ballroom; it is the Basie orchestra with
Jo Jones on drums and Billie Holiday singing. The groove is vicious,
menacing; as the band restrains itself for the first chorus and then
gradually turns it on, the guitarist Freddie Green drives the rhythm,
chunk-chunk-chunk, and Holiday phrases way behind the beat.

"Ra-rin to go, and there ain't nobody gonna hold me down," she
sings. Haynes, wearing velvet pants and cowboy boots, sat on his
living-room sofa and crouched close to the speaker to hear the details. "Can I hear that little part again?" he said. "I thought I heard
a cowbell."

He did. Jones hits the cowbell three times at the start of the second chorus, linking the bars together. From that point the band surges a little, makes the song meaner. "Aaah-haaa!" Haynes hollered.

"That's a hell of a one to start with, man," said Haynes, shaking his head. "If anybody wants to know what swing is, check that out. Everybody's in the pocket. You know, you just feel it: I see people dancing."

Haynes played with three masterful singers: Sarah Vaughan, Ella Fitzgerald, and Billie Holiday. His time with Holiday came during her last run at a club—Storyville, in Boston, in 1959. Late Holiday is different. It communicates frailty; it's not rhythmically invincible, like this. "But there were still nights when some of *that* feeling was there," he said. (It's true; on the surviving radio broadcasts of Holiday's shows from that week, you can hear him help to trigger that feeling with his drumming.)

He was born in Roxbury, Massachusetts. His parents had moved from Barbados, and his father had a job at Standard Oil. There were a lot of jazz bands in Boston but, according to Haynes, few good drummers. One of them, Herbert Wright, lived across the way from the Haynes house, on Haskins Street. He played drums with James Reese Europe and gave Haynes a few lessons in playing paradiddles. (Later, he earned the distinction of reportedly stabbing Europe to death in a fight.)

Haynes grew up among four smart, accomplished brothers. One was Michael Haynes, who has been a pastor at Roxbury's Twelfth Baptist Church since 1964, in addition to serving as a Massachusetts state representative from 1965 to 1970. Michael was close to Dr. Martin Luther King, Jr., befriending him while King was studying for his doctorate in Boston. Another brother was C. Vincent Haynes, a photographer and writer, who died in 2002.

His brother Douglas Haynes was a trumpet player who attended the New England Conservatory of Music after serving in the army; he traveled to New York City when Roy was still in high school, and came to know musicians socially at the Savoy Ballroom. He introduced Roy to a number of them, including Papa Jo Jones, one night at the Southland Café, before Haynes left Boston in 1945 to work in New York himself.

Haynes's next choice was "Queer Street," again by Basie. "There was a White Castle, a hamburger joint, on Broadway and Forty-seventh Street," he remembered, as the song played. "They had a jukebox there. I would put dimes in, and keep playing it over and over." What he wanted to hear, he said, was Shadow Wilson's complicated two-bar fill on the snare drum near the end of the song.

The tune is sharp Harlem-ballroom swing from right after the war—1946—with huge dynamic shifts and a deep four-four bass line. During the last fifteen seconds of the three-minute piece, Wilson comes in, playing double-time drum rolls and then turning his beat around. "Ohh, that's it," Haynes said, looking happy, and momentarily dazed. "Man, that's something. Like I'm twenty years old listening to that."

Wilson later played, off and on, in a short-lived quartet with Thelonious Monk and John Coltrane, the group that famously occupied the Five Spot Café for the second half of 1957, when Coltrane began to realize his own potential. "But I took him as a big-band drummer," Haynes said.

"At one point, I was with Luis Russell," he remembered. (This would have been in the mid-1940s.) "We were playing in Detroit, and Illinois Jacquet was in town, too." After the gig, the Russell band went to see Jacquet, who was a star then. "I was good for sitting in with anyone I wanted to, mainly saxophone players," he said. "I was known to be able to swing. Anyway, Shadow Wilson was the drummer that night. Shadow must have called on me, because I wouldn't have asked him to let me sit in—I don't think I was *that* game. But I went and played, and Jacquet didn't know. When he turned around, it was me. He often talked about that. Because"—he hissed—"Shadow *could swing.* He didn't *have* to play no solo.

"And I sort of fell into that category, too," he added, with an if-I-do-say-so-myself tone. "I was known to be able to swing. That's one of the things that I'm sure carried me in this business this long—having *that* thing. I talked to my grandson about it."

Haynes's grandson, the son of his daughter Leslie, is the drummer Marcus Gilmore—now in his early twenties, but a knockout musician even at eighteen. In some ways, Haynes sees his life relived in his grandson's. Gilmore was born in a house in Queens that Haynes had bought. While studying at the Manhattan School of Music, he lived in a Morningside Heights dorm building next door to where Haynes lived when he played with Charlie Parker in the 1950s. And as Haynes was in the 1950s and '60s, Gilmore is a stylebook of outward and sophisticated new jazz drumming.

What are the drummers from Marcus's generation doing differently from those of yours? I asked Haynes.

"Oh, they're doing a lot of stuff different," he said.

But what? I pressed. For instance, in the 1940s and '50s, there was a bottom-line responsibility to swing hard. Is that still as important as it was?

"That's a funny word. What did you just say?"

Responsibility?

"No, what did you just say after that?"

To swing hard.

"No, it wasn't necessarily to swing hard. I was with Stan Getz for a while, and you know, it wasn't particularly hard swinging. Sarah, for five years. We did some big-band stuff, too, but it was light. A lot of it was just mellow swinging. I played with Lennie Tristano and Lester Young, who were not exactly hard swingers. Though there were nights," he considered. "I would say Art Blakey would be more *hard*. And Elvin Jones maybe would be more hard. So I did that if the situation called for it."

That matter defused, he answered the original question. "But what are they doing different now? Mmm, they're studying more, to start with, whereas people like myself, most of our studying was on the bandstand. And drummers now—not only drummers but players in general—they talk. There's more talk, discussing what they're doing and how they do what they do—theory. There are more drummers today than there were during the period when I was coming up, the forties and fifties. I don't know what I would do if I was just a youngster coming up now. Even sometimes when you go to Europe now, they're becoming more Americanized; they want to do the same type of thing that's being done here."

Max Roach was born two years before Haynes; they were important drummers in bebop's first wave. "When I heard Max the first time," Haynes recalled, "I said to myself, 'He loves Jo Jones too.'"

We listened to Coleman Hawkins's recording from February 1944 of "Woody'n You," written by Dizzy Gillespie. It is considered the first bebop recording session. Gillespie is in the group, and Max Roach is the drummer. "I was impressed," he said about Roach. "It was like he was talking to me."

Haynes especially identified one detail: as Hawkins finishes his first solo in "Woody'n You," Roach makes the final beat of the bar part of a figure that enjoins the bar with the next, and also the next chorus of the song. It sounds like *one TWO three FOUR ONE BOOM three FOUR one TWO three FOUR*. It breaks up the flow of time; it creates tension, and it stabilizes, too. Later in the song, during a trumpet solo, Roach thuds the bass drum, creating a single offbeat palpitation in the middle of a bar. "There," Haynes said.

Bebop was just beginning to take over then, and Haynes stood at the middle of it. He saw some older musicians' dissatisfaction with the way jazz was changing then—becoming more melodically fractured, more staccato, more drum-centered. Roy Eldridge was one, he remembered.

But from 1947 to 1949, Haynes played with Lester Young, the paradigmatic soloist of the period before bebop, and had no problem. "I had heard Lester didn't like people getting too involved," he said. "But he liked the way I was getting involved. I was dancing with him from up here," he said, holding his hand up at the level of his head—meaning the ride cymbal. "I was doing stuff with my left hand and right foot, too, but I was always feeding him that thing from up there. I was swinging with him. And the word that you used earlier—*hard*—it wasn't particularly hard. We were *moving*, you know, trying to paint a picture."

He did something similar with John Coltrane, when he filled in for Elvin Jones in the John Coltrane Quartet in 1961 and 1963. After you become used to Jones's drumming in the Coltrane group, hearing Haynes is a big difference; since the emphasis pulls away from the bass drum and toward the snare and cymbals, you can hear the bass and piano more.

Despite his protests against being known as a hard-swinging drummer, Haynes has always been a forceful one. I wondered whether each time he started with some new bandleader during those early years—whether Miles Davis, Charlie Parker, Kai Winding, or whoever else—he felt an instinct to see how much he could get away with, musically, before they started pushing back or objecting.

"No, I didn't think that way at all," he said. "Whoever I was playing with, I think they probably wanted me for what I was trying to do."

The photographer Lee Friedlander, who visited Haynes with me that day, asked him if he knew a ten-inch instructional record from the 1940s by Baby Dodds, the early New Orleans jazz drummer.

"Yeah, man." Haynes smiled. "I used to travel with that record."

The record contains "Playing for the Benefit of the Band," a wise and trenchant lecture. In it, Dodds says:

> Anybody can beat a drum, but anybody can't drum. You must study those things—study a guy's human nature. Study what he will take or what he will go for . . . that's why all guys is not drummers that's drumming.
>
> For a fact, you got to use diplomacy. You must use that. You got to study something that will make them work. You can't holler at a man, you can't dog him. Not in music. It's up to me to keep all that lively. That's my job . . . There's more beside drumming than just beating. It's my job to know what

that part is—I got to find it. When I sit down in a band, that I hunts for . . . I find the kick to send 'em off with.

. . . You see a band dead: a drummer can liven up everybody, make everybody have a different spirit. And he can make everybody pretty angry, too. And he can have 'em so that they be so angry with him, but they have to play.

"We've grown a lot since then," Haynes said, speaking for all drummers. "Baby Dodds said he would want to know what tunes his band was going to play, and the guys in the band would say, 'What do you care? You're only the drummer.' Shit. Makes a difference, man."

It has become almost a cliché to compare Haynes's improvising to the sound of the timbales player in a Latin band, but he has never talked very specifically about Latin music. He told me that he used to be friends with Ubaldo Nieto, the *timbalero* from Machito's orchestra. I suggested that we listen together to Machito's "Tanga," recorded at Birdland in 1951.

This "Tanga" changes its atmosphere several times, through switches of key or tension building from different sections of the bandstand. Then suddenly the entire governing language alters. Cuban rhythm becomes swing; you hear a drum kit and cymbals instead of conga and timbales, and Zoot Sims starts playing a jazz tenor saxophone solo. Haynes confirmed that it was Nieto, changing over to a drum kit midsong.

"We were always playing opposite Machito in Birdland in those years," he said. "And I always did like the sound of timbales, the approach. Sometimes when I'd play my solos, I'd approach the traps with that same effect, like when I hit rim shots," catching the head and the rim of the drum at the same time. "A lot of the older gentlemen, like Chick Webb and Papa Jo, they did rim shots too. But doing it with no snares on, with that tom-tom sort of Afro-Cuban feeling, I always liked that. So lots of times my solo would be sort of patterned on that style of playing. On one record I did called *We Three*, with Phineas Newborn and Paul Chambers, I'm playing the high hat with a sort of beat that Uba would play." (The recording is from 1958, and the song is "Reflection.")

Finally we listened to Sarah Vaughan singing "Lover Man," from 1945, with Dizzy Gillespie and Charlie Parker. (The drummer is Sid Catlett.) It wasn't what Haynes expected; it is what he called a walking ballad, but not as extravagantly slow as the kind he had in mind, the version he recorded with Vaughan in 1954.

Haynes loved the five years he worked with Vaughan. She had impeccable timing, heard well enough to correct a bass player's chord changes, and filled in on piano when necessary. She sang virtuosically on stage and hung out virtuosically afterward. Haynes suffered his first hangover after going to an after-hours bar with her. (It was Philadelphia, 1953, and Gordon's gin.)

"She sang some of the slowest ballads, probably, in the world," he said. "And in the fifties, we had bass players like Joe Benjamin. Bass players in those days had a way of letting the notes ring out. We don't get that with a lot of young bass players today. Musicians used to say that Joe Benjamin was like a whole band. He could make a sound last—instead of saying *boomp, boomp, boomp,* like a thumper, thumping on the bass instead of drawing out the beauty in the instrument—he would play *BOOOOM, BOOOOM, BOOOOM.*

"With drumming, there was an art to playing it and making it sustained, making it sound full with brushes. But you've got to have the right rhythm section to make it sound effective. And we did, every night. Moment by moment, there was always something musical happening," he said.

"To have played with all the people we're talking about? Jesus Christ. When I go through it, I'm reliving everything I'm talking about. It feels like a dream, going back."

He had talked about Billie Holiday and Sarah Vaughan. What about Ella Fitzgerald?

"I played with Ella Fitzgerald for the whole summer of 1952," he said. "That was hard. It wasn't like playing with Sarah. Hank Jones was the pianist, and Nelson Boyd was the bassist. It was like playing with a big band; she had a lot of energy, and she could swing. One night we played in Rhode Island, a club. That weekend, opening up, they had one of those organ trios. Now, this organ trio was on fire. And after that, Ella said to us, 'Y'all are not swinging.' Can you imagine me and Hank Jones on the bandstand not swinging?

"But it's understandable. She was feeling the threat of having that organ trio opposite her. She was a beautiful person; she'd give you good money. I remember one night we played outside of Baltimore, Sparrows Beach—that's where all the black people could go, because they couldn't go to a lot of other beaches in D.C. or Baltimore. We did a gig there on Sunday afternoon. Her driver's nickname was Mississippi. He drove us from New York, in her Cadillac, to Baltimore. Coming back, we had a gig that night in Harlem, at a place called the Renaissance. Traffic was backed up all the way from Maryland to New York. When we got to New York, it was twelve midnight. She sat in the car and cried; she said it was the first time she ever missed a gig. And gave us some money anyhow."

It is the time he spent with Vaughan—1953 to 1958—that he rates highest. "The audiences were *dressed*," he remembered. "People were respecting the music. Not that they didn't respect it when I played with Bird, but sometimes you didn't know whether he was going to show up, or whatever. The musicianship during those years, the places we played—it was enjoyable. Plus I got a check every week. And during that period, man, her voice was . . . *mmm*. That shit was uncanny.

"And that was the first time I ever went to Europe. In Paris, we played with Coleman Hawkins and Illinois Jacquet on the same show. I backed up Coleman. And that was the first time I ever had my picture on the cover of a magazine. In *Paris*."

Set List

Count Basie, "Swing, Brother, Swing," from *America's #1 Band!: The Columbia Years* (Sony Legacy), recorded 1937.

Count Basie, "Queer Street," from *America's #1 Band!*, recorded 1946.

Coleman Hawkins, "Woody'n You," from *Rainbow Mist* (Delmark), recorded 1944.

Machito and His Afro-Cubans, "Tanga," from *Carambola* (Tumbao), recorded 1951.

Dizzy Gillespie, "Lover Man" (with Sarah Vaughan), from *Odyssey: 1945–52* (Savoy Jazz), recorded 1945.

13

Head to Toes

Paul Motian

The drummer Paul Motian doesn't get on airplanes anymore. Once, in the mid-1990s, he took a three-week tour involving thirty-five flights. By 2003, he was booking himself with three different bands all over Europe and Japan. Soon after, he decided he was sick of traveling.

It's not just long distances. "I don't even go to New Jersey or Brooklyn anymore, man," he said defiantly on one rainy October day in 2005, looking toward the Hudson River from the window of his Manhattan apartment.

He was seventy-four and had lived in the same spot for nearly forty years, most of that time alone. In his working life, Motian wanted one thing above all: to hear his own drum sound clearly. He found that in the windowless, wedge-shaped enclosure of the Village Vanguard, he can.

His is an unusual sound, which does not limit any part of the drum set to a particular role. Motian has two ride cymbals, one of which he has been playing since the 1950s; he gets a dark, nuanced sound from it. He uses no padding or muffling in his twenty-inch bass drum, and with it he can get a deep, loud, loose noise, almost a splat—a reminder that a bass drum is an instrument of emphasis, not just timekeeping. He uses nylon brushes, quieter than wire ones.

I have seen him play most of the way through "Body and Soul" with no bass drum at all—just one brush on a cymbal, *ching-ching-a-ching,* and the other, only at the end, lightly rustling on a snare drum, for color rather than rhythm. In general, he plays whatever moves into his imagination. Four of his beats could be marked by a few snare-drum hits, a few clenches of the high hat, and a couple of combinations; in the next bar, he might play small military rolls and one lone cymbal crash.

He works mostly with three of his own groups: his trio with the guitarist Bill Frisell and the saxophonist Joe Lovano, which has grown steadily more influential over two decades; the changeable Trio 2000+1, with the bassist Larry Grenadier and either Chris Potter or Bill McHenry on saxophone (the plus-one being the enigmatic Japanese pianist Masabumi Kikuchi, the singer Rebecca Martin, or others); and the group formerly known as the Electric Bebop Band, which became the Paul Motian Band in 2006, and works within an odd structure of three guitarists, two tenor saxophonists, bass, and drums.

Small and bald, with excellent posture—he runs a few miles in Central Park, which neighbors his apartment, nearly every day—Motian practices rapid, streetwise self-deprecation, cussing constantly. That, and a nail-gun laugh, give him the demeanor of an old-school hipster. He is the kind of person who wears sunglasses indoors after 11:00 p.m. and calls a room full of people, at one time, "man." (As in "Hey, thanks for coming, man!") But he can't be reduced that easily. History has shaken him out as one of the greatest drummers in all of jazz—a select group that would include his own favorite drummers: Baby Dodds, Sid Catlett, Philly Joe Jones, Max Roach.

Motian's playing moves beyond the styles particularly associated with any era of jazz. Spare and never facile, his constant run of improvisation can seem to get beyond thinking. At the moments of his highest musical abstraction, there is great sensitivity, and always the implication of a pulse. Jazz, mostly, is about testing the integrity of a song's frame. Motian appears to believe that if you truly respect the frame, you can put anything inside it.

Original compositions tend to take up about half of his sets. An amateur pianist since his tenure as the drummer in Keith Jarrett's quartet during the late 1960s and '70s, he has written dozens of excellent melodies, flowing and terse. (The other half generally consists of tunes by jazz composers he admires, Thelonious Monk or Bud Powell or Charles Mingus, or popular standards.) He doesn't overcompose; he likes hearing his music liberally interpreted and lets his band members do what they want.

Motian does not advance any great theories about his style. One day in the mid-1980s, after an uncountable number of different experiences playing with Motian, the pianist Paul Bley suddenly had a moment of clarity. "Oh, now I get it," he told the drummer. "You play ideas."

Do you? I asked Motian.

"I don't know," he answered, in his chalky voice. "When he said that, I thought, 'Oh, maybe that's what I do.'"

Another day, during a recording session in 2004, Hank Jones, the wise old pianist, took him aside. "I know your secret," he whispered. Motian told this story with a baffled shrug. "I wish I knew what he meant," he said. "Wow!"

He came up with a fantastically judicious list of music to listen to. He kept claiming not to have an aptitude for thinking about music analytically. Later it became clear that he knew exactly what he wanted to talk about.

Motian grew up in Providence, Rhode Island, hearing big bands downtown at the Metropolitan Theater and at Rhodes on the Pawtuxet, a dance space just outside the city. He entered the navy in 1950 during the Korean War, considering it a better option than being drafted into the army. That decision enabled him to attend the Navy School of Music in Washington, which he attended briefly and remembers as "a farce."

He sailed around the Mediterranean for two and a half years in the admiral's band of the Seventh Fleet and then was stationed in Brooklyn in the fall of 1953. Discharged a year later, he moved to Ninth Street in the East Village. His share of the rent was $12.50 a month. He collected unemployment, ate potato knishes, and played at jam sessions.

The first piece Motian wanted to hear connected to his days of playing marches in the navy. It is from Baby Dodds's *Talking and Drum Solos*, one of several documentary records he made in the 1940s.* Dodds, the great New Orleans drummer of the 1920s and '30s, worked with Louis Armstrong, Jelly Roll Morton, and Johnny

---

* This is a different Baby Dodds record from the one Roy Haynes talked about in the preceding chapter. That was a ten-inch record on American Music, called *Baby Dodds no. 3.*

Dodds, his brother; his career had a second wind in New York City during the 1940s Dixieland revival.

The ten-inch record, on which Dodds also discusses his history and technique, is a primer on different rhythms for different drums. Cueing up the record on his turntable, Motian started with Dodds's solo version of the traditional New Orleans march tune "Maryland." He singled it out not to talk about surface flash, technique, or speed; he just wanted to show how, while playing a march rhythm on the snare drum all the way through, Dodds delineates the verse from the bridge by pumping a bass drum on the bridge but not on the verses. That was all.

"I guess my point is that it makes a difference," Motian said. "He's in a different part of the song."

What about that cymbal sound? I asked. The one tap at the end of each section. Why is it so soft? Was Dodds, who worked during the earliest days of jazz recording, just respecting the sensitivity of the microphones? "No, I don't think so," Motian replied. "You know, the drummers in those days—I don't think they bashed the cymbals like they do now. It's delicate. It's a cymbal, man. It's not a jackhammer."

He took the needle off the record. "The first drum set I had was made during World War II. It didn't even have metal. It had wooden rims. My drum sound was closer to that than it is to my sound now. I wasn't that aware of sound. Not like I am now."

In 1955 Motian met the pianist Bill Evans. A few years later Evans formed his own trio, with Motian and eventually Scott LaFaro on bass, which destabilized the pyramid structure of the normal piano trio, increasing the mobility of the bassist and drummer around the leader. Among their recordings were a few genuine twentieth-century landmarks, *Sunday at the Village Vanguard* and *Waltz for Debby*. Motian loved the group, especially with LaFaro involved, and it was steady work; his diaries from 1962 show that he played twenty-five and a half weeks with Evans that year.

That period, the late '50s and early '60s, before he graduated to being a bandleader, was the busiest of his life. As he talked about it, he brought out one of his date books from that time, from the year 1958. The pages were crowded with musicians' names, phone numbers, and the amount he earned for each club or studio job. A sideman's well-kept date book is valuable to jazz. It tells everything that isn't glorious enough to be wrongly understood: quickly disappearing bands, failed jazz clubs, average pay scales.

Two weeks with Lee Konitz: the book had it that Motian earned $125 for the first week, $135 for the second. "A lot," he said, surprised. "Usually I remember a week's pay was like, ninety or a hundred dollars." A recording session with Warne Marsh and Paul Chambers, produced by Lennie Tristano: $34.64.

On another page, in Motian's careful hand: "The Enchanted Room." "I don't know where that was, man," he said. "Where was that?"

In 1958, he had played in Tony Scott's band, with Sam Jones on bass, Jimmy Knepper on trombone, Kenny Burrell on guitar, at a club called the Black Pearl. "It was on the East Side, in the seventies," Motian remembered. "Ten p.m. to four a.m." Billie Holiday sang a few tunes. "I remember she had on a fur coat. I think she kept it on while she sang. Ha, ha! But you know, Tony Scott forced her to sing. She didn't want to sing. Tony Scott said, 'Ladies and gentlemen, Billie Holiday! Give her a hand!' She's shaking her head. But Tony Scott was just too insistent."

In 1964 and '65, he worked with the singer and pianist Mose Allison quite a bit. During a three-week gig at Birdland in January 1965, Allison's trio played on a double bill with the John Coltrane Quartet. One of those nights, Motian sat in for Coltrane's drummer, Elvin Jones, who couldn't make it to the club. Coltrane liked him, and they talked after the show. "Where are you going next with Mose?" Coltrane asked. "Oh, Mose doesn't travel with us," Motian answered. "He hires his own bands wherever he goes. It's easier for him to gig around that way." "I wish I could do that," Coltrane told him, to Motian's great surprise. (Coltrane's quartet, at the time, was the greatest small group in jazz.)

A few pages later: *Too bad, I've got to work*. "Look at that. I wanted a day off," he said, commiserating with his old self. *Anniversary*. "Yeah, I was married. That was the first anniversary of our marriage. What does that say?" *Tomorrow is my wife's birthday*. "Ha, ha!" He quieted. "She's long gone." It was Motian's only marriage, and it ended in divorce; she died in 1980.

Motian played with many other bandleaders too in that period: Stan Getz, Lennie Tristano, Martial Solal, Zoot Sims, Eddie Costa, Johnny Griffin, and even with Tony Martin, the actor and romantic singer. For one week in Boston, in 1960, Motian got to play with Thelonious Monk. (Elvin Jones was supposed to be the drummer, but he went missing.)

Motian chose Monk's version of "Carolina Moon," an old waltz which had been commonly understood as cornpone. Monk rethought it when he recorded it in 1952. He plays the end of the waltz melody as a short piano introduction, and then bass and drums crash in, playing a speedy 4/4. In the middle of the tune the drummer, Max Roach, slows down to midtempo 4/4, but the soloists, Lou Donaldson, Kenny Dorham, and Lucky Thompson, continue to play in waltz time. Listening to it, he turned on like a lamp. He didn't have much to say; instead, he clapped and counted all the way through, laughing.

Monk was an easy boss. He paid Motian two hundred dollars for the week, good wages, and didn't demand much. One night he asked Motian to sing him his cymbal beat. He did, and Monk thought about it and sang a corrected version back to him, with a tiny bit more emphasis on the last stroke of the triplet.

Next was Big Sid Catlett, the great swing drummer. We heard "I Found a New Baby," from 1944, on one of the few sessions that Catlett led during his life. It's a drummer's showpiece, with three different drum-solo breaks; it forms an essay on the ecstasy and flexibility of 4/4 swing. But the remarkable thing is that the action of the song is nearly all located on the snare drum.

The other remarkable thing, to Motian, is that Catlett plays variations on the melody with his drums. You can hear the song in his drum breaks. Catlett plays the first chorus-length solo (thirty-two bars) with brushes, and the second (thirty-two bars) and third (eight bars) with sticks; he keeps raising the stakes so that three-quarters of the last solo is one continuous, propulsive, clattering roll.

"That's great, man," Motian said, as soon as the track stopped. "It's mostly snare drum—once in a while he hits a tom-tom. I don't know about that tom-tom—it's sort of a dead kind of sound. But that's the way they'd use them in those days. The bass drum is almost exactly the kind of sound Max Roach had—that muffled sound. I mean, I don't have anything against it. But it's not what I would do. I want to play that again." He cackled.

We heard it for a second time. "It sounds like it's simple and easy," he said, as it ended. "I don't know why I keep saying this, but it's like talking. The last eight that he played . . ." Orally he imitated the roll, then the light, dancing figure in the fourth bar. "Drummers that play now—I haven't heard that many, but it seems like they want to beat the shit out of the drum. Full of technique. Who was it—Lester Young?—who said, 'Yeah, man, that's great. But what's your story? What are you saying?'"

Max Roach used to live a few blocks away from Motian on Central Park West and has long been one of his idols. (Roach, who died in 2007, was seven years older.) When Motian joined the New York jazz scene, in 1955, Roach, who was the great drummer of bebop's first wave, was already taking that music into a new territory with the Clifford Brown–Max Roach Quintet.

Motian saw the band play a lot. "I went to hear them once," he said of that group, "and I think Sonny Rollins was on tenor. I was with this bass player I used to play with a lot, Al Cotton, and he said: 'Look at Max. Watch: when he's playing, he uses his whole body. He's exercising when he's playing. He's moving around. He's not just sitting there. It's not just in the wrist, in the hands. It's the whole body.'

"I'm talking about the midfifties, when I got turned on to that: the drums and me should be one thing, you know. It's part of me. From head to fingernails to the end of my toes, man. The drums, it's all me."

He wanted to hear the Victor Young movie theme "Delilah," a midtempo minor-key ballad, from the Brown-Roach band's first album, recorded in 1954. It has incredible clarity; the definition of each section makes it shine like a hit pop song. "It's so organized, man," Motian said. "Arranged so beautiful. Simple, but great. Nice bass drum sound," he said. It was that muffled sound, though, that he had just been referring to. "Well, it's not what I would do, but it's nice. Very nicely tuned, nice intervals, nice sound."

Did he get to know Roach right away when he got to New York? "Not really. Except one time, when I was playing at the Half Note with Tony Scott, and he had to use my drums. At that time, it was like a white-pearl drum set made by a company called Leedy. And in those days, I used to tune the drums really taut, high-pitched. I had to make every stroke. Anyway, my drums were on the stage, but I was late for the gig, and Max Roach was there. He played the set for me, on my drums. When I came in, he said to me, 'Man, your drums are really hard to play.' The drums are easier to play when they're loose. You can fake stuff."

There's a Max Roach solo in the middle of "Delilah," for an entire chorus. Just as Baby Dodds did—and just as Sid Catlett did—Roach indicates the structure of the melody in his solo, changing his patterns to mark its divisions. I suggested that a thread was emerging here, kind of an unusual one. He smiled a little bit and raised one eyebrow and kept talking. "He plays different sections of a song, he points it out to you. No confusion at all. You know what I mean?"

Kenny Clarke and Max Roach were the first great drummers of bebop, lining out the pulse on the ride cymbal rather than the bass drum; suddenly, jazz drumming became higher pitched and more flexible. Motian idolized Clarke, as well. He saw Clarke play many times at the Café Bohemia in the West Village, before the elder drummer resettled in France in 1956; later, Motian got to know him in Paris in the early 1980s, a few years before Clarke died.

Clarke played with a Miles Davis group for the 1957 soundtrack to the Louis Malle film noir *Ascenseur pour l'echafaud* (*Elevator to the Gallows)*, and Motian, only in recent years, has become partial to the record. "I was in a restaurant," he said, "and they were playing this on the music system. Blew me away, right?" He knew it was Miles Davis, but he didn't know what album it came from; he bought five different Miles Davis records before he realized it might be from the movie. We listened to "Motel," a fast trio improvisation with trumpet, bass, and drums, based on the chords of "Sweet Georgia Brown." Clarke plays with brushes on a snare drum, varying his patterns within the same rhythm all the way through. There's not one cymbal crash, no bass drum. For a musician who likes to boil things down, it is justification.

"Just to get so much music and so much feeling and so much swing from the minimum amount of drums, man; that's incredible," Motian said. "Just that beat. You can't get any better than that, I don't think. There's so much music there, just on a snare drum. It's like a symphony to me."

Set List

Baby Dodds, "Maryland" and "Tom Tom Workout," from *Talking and Drum Solos* (Atavistic Unheard Music Series), recorded 1946–1954.

Thelonious Monk, "Carolina Moon," from *Genius of Modern Music,* vol. 2 (Blue Note), recorded 1952.

Sid Catlett, "I Found a New Baby," from *Sid Catlett, 1944–46* (Classics), recorded 1944.

Clifford Brown and Max Roach, "Delilah," from *Clifford Brown and Max Roach* (Verve), recorded 1954.

Miles Davis, "Motel," from *Ascenseur pour l'echafaud* (*Elevator to the Gallows*), original soundtrack (Verve), recorded 1957.

14

A Million Just Like It

Branford Marsalis

In September 2006, Hurricane Ernesto was drawing close to Durham, North Carolina. Among other things, this meant that Branford Marsalis wasn't going to play golf. Around eleven in the morning, he came to the door of his tract mansion in his T-shirt, shorts, and socks. He was alone and preoccupied by the fact that his wife and two of his children were stuck in an airport in Sweden, their flight delayed for five hours because of an unrelated maintenance problem.

A saxophone was out, and the television was on. He had been practicing while watching an action movie. "You know this? *Siege*? Denzel and Bruce Willis. Terrorist shit."

He had lived in the house, in a housing complex built next to one of the better golf courses in North Carolina, since 2001. Previously Marsalis had lived in New Rochelle, New York, and Brooklyn, but moved south to remove his family, especially his son Reese, from what he defined as a particularly East Coast sense of entitlement. "I'm in a place now where all I can focus on is bettering myself," he said. "There's no distractions. I listen to music all day." Having heard similar reports, I thought it would be a good time for me to visit and listen to some with him.

Branford is the eldest of the six Marsalis brothers, four of whom are in jazz: himself; his brother Wynton, the trumpeter and major-domo of Jazz at Lincoln Center; Delfeayo, the trombonist and record producer; and Jason, the drummer. He came to be known, initially, as the tenor player alongside Wynton in Art Blakey's Jazz Messengers in 1980, and subsequently as part of Wynton's band, making records like *Think of One* and *Black Codes from the Underground*.

A side benefit of the move to North Carolina was greater concentration on his own work. It has been a generative period, with the establishment of his own record label (Marsalis Music) and an artist-in-residency job for himself and his band at North Carolina Central University, a historically black college in Durham. Since moving south, he and his wife, Nicole, also had two more children, both girls: Peyton and Thaïs.

He also gave up the idea of being part of the pop-culture mainstream, which had been part of his agenda when he entered the Berklee College of Music in 1981, wanting to be a producer after the models of Quincy Jones and George Martin. It was part of his agenda again, after a few years of receiving excessive (and, he believes, thoroughly undeserved) amounts of praise as one of jazz's "young lions," when he joined Sting's band for two years in the mid-1980s; and again when he led the band on *The Tonight Show with Jay Leno* from 1992 to 1995, thereby becoming a Famous Person.

It is not easy for him to leave this point, his pop-culture apostasy, unexamined. Marsalis is an opinionated sort. Twenty years ago, those opinions could be loud and grating; now there is a more weathered and empathetic feeling about them, but they still arrive about one per sentence, and they have become more idiosyncratic, almost wild. His arts-administrator brother Wynton is a straight talker as well, but Branford represents nobody but himself. Especially in his big, staid house, surrounded by the culture of southern bonhomie and perfect fairways, he is appealingly manic.

One of the most revealing things Marsalis said came at the end of the day. Ever since his days studying saxophone at Berklee, he has been a Coltrane fiend, so I had brought something good I thought he would want to copy, an unissued live Coltrane recording from Chicago in 1961, a blues variously called "Coltrane Blues" or "Vierd Blues" or "John Paul Jones." It's Coltrane after "Giant Steps" and his long tunnel of harmonic study, after he gave up his obsession with patterns, when he was just beginning to sound monstrous, and when McCoy Tyner and Elvin Jones had fully settled into his group. The audio quality is passable, but the performance is lethal.

Marsalis listened and cheered by reflex, as if he were at a ball game. "Whoo! Swing, baby. Ohhh!" Then he shook his head, making a complicated face.

"My friends would never understand this. And they shouldn't. It's for us to understand and enjoy and love, and the hell with the rest of it. The whole self-aggrandizing stance might get you some attention, but in my mind I've checked out on that whole thing. I moved here. I'm done. I just want to play. I don't want to be in magazines."

* * *

Perhaps as a consequence of this attitude, his own band, the Branford Marsalis Quartet, has improved. In the late 1990s, getting its bearings after the death of Marsalis's previous pianist, Kenny Kirkland, it had the potential to be one of the best small groups in jazz. But more recently it truly has become that, a bullish, competitive band that acts as a standard-bearer of modern mainstream jazz, its music harder and more truculent—and, at the same time, more detailed—than many listeners think they can reasonably expect from straight-ahead jazz.

This particular lineup has stayed intact since 1999, with the pianist Joey Calderazzo, the bassist Eric Revis, and the drummer Jeff "Tain" Watts. Its record *Braggtown*, released in 2006 just before my visit, ranges from hurtling Coltrane-ish music to mournful and slow ballads, as well as a version of "O Solitude," a song written by the seventeenth-century English composer Henry Purcell.

Marsalis is fascinated by slow music; he also has recorded an album of crawl-tempo ballads called *Eternal*. "I'm listening to a lot of lieder right now," he said, "because I like the idea that you can write songs with a certain amount of emotional content, especially when you don't know what the lyrics say. From happy to sad to wistful to melancholy." Most of the music, in fact, that had been beguiling him around this time was classical music—Peter Lieberson's *Neruda Songs*, for example—and he was trying to puzzle out a way of bringing some form of melodic craftsmanship into a jazz group without making it seem forced or soigné-stupid. ("I hear it in my head, but I can't express it yet," he said later.)

Though he prides himself on the lack of distractions in his new life, he found some anyway during our interview, including the *New York Times* crossword puzzle—it was a Wednesday—and his e-mail. He tended to them while talking almost nonstop for five hours, occasionally springing up and sliding across the wooden floor in his socks to cue a new piece of music on his CD player or his iPod.

The causes of his excitement tended to be pieces of music that were very long or slow or dense. Marsalis is almost compulsive about sharing knowledge, but he never did what snobs do, which is to claim his enthusiasms as innate. He was always waking up to something big, it seemed, and discovering what he had been missing. This trait may be a midlife cliché, but it's not a bad one for a musician to have.

First he found a CD called *Fun with Bing and Louis*, a recording of performances on Bing Crosby's radio program by Crosby and Louis Armstrong. He mentioned that it contained a piece he'd been playing for his students at North Carolina Central. "I make them listen to nothing but thirties and forties music, which they hate," he said, grimly. "I say, 'You guys have to understand American dance culture of the thirties and forties, the pulse of dance music, to understand this music the right way.' But they all have fake-books"— meaning lead-sheet books, designed to get a musician performing a song quickly, if sometimes without the nuances—"and they all want to play . . ." He searched for the right hard-bop standard to use as a negative example. " 'Blues-ette.' It's like, *no, no, no*."

This was the beginning of Marsalis's hammer-blow opinions. Like his musician brothers, he believes in standards of quality, and his standards, at least from one day to the next, if not always one year to the next, are fixed. One of his more vociferous tough-love beliefs is that jazz occupies precisely the level of exposure it deserves, given the way it has come to be understood and per-formed.

"Musicians are always talking about, 'Why isn't jazz popular?'" he said. "But musicians today"—he was talking specifically about jazz musicians—"are completely devoid of charisma. People never really liked the music in the first place. So now you have musicians who are proficient at playing instruments, and really, really smart, and know a lot of music, and people sit there and it's just boring to them—because they're trying to *see* something, or feel it."

We listened to a very short version of "Up a Lazy River," from March 16, 1949, in which Armstrong sings, scatting and trading vocal and instrumental phrases with Jack Teagarden, and then playing a little trumpet at the end. This was one of their practiced numbers, leaking with high musicality and comic flash. At one point, leaning into a phrase, Armstrong sings *"oohriver"*—not really a joke, but just a kind of counterpoint to himself—and the studio audience cracks up.

"It's really interesting," Marsalis said. "Even in parts where Armstrong isn't doing anything particularly comedic, people start laughing, because of his body language and the way he gets notes out. Americans see everything first and hear it second. The idea that the music they're listening to could be supergenius is *completely* second. They're laughing, while he's just singing."

He admired Armstrong's chromatic run of notes at the end, but he wanted to talk about simpler things. "One of the things I like about all the swing music is the songs that they picked didn't rely on heavy amounts of harmony," he said. "What they relied on more was a really strong melodic sense and a certain level of charisma to pull the song off."

He played the song again and focused on Armstrong's vocal solo, which starts after the first eight bars. "What he was singing—that's a solo. If I play that as a solo, people say, 'That's *bad*, where'd you get that from?' Check it out." Marsalis sang along to a mellow, linear, melodic part of the improvisation. "Sounds like Lester Young." He sang along to the more exaggerated, note-smearing part which immediately follows. "If you can play that, man, people will go *nuts*."

He found another Armstrong-Teagarden track, "Rockin' Chair," a studio recording from 1947, with a slow, comfortable tempo; at the beginning, Teagarden sings, and Armstrong answers each line, vocally. "The singing and the trumpet playing are inextricably bound together," he said of Armstrong. Then the musicians switched places, with Teagarden answering Armstrong's lines. "But when the other guy tries to be the interlocutor?" He blew a raspberry. "He's a good straight man, but he can't do the other thing. It's canned.

"See," he continued, talking about Armstrong, "he has it all in his head. He hears the sound; he hears the things that go against the groove; he drops the flat-fives in there wherever he wants. He can express the song in a conversational way. A lot of other guys, at the time and even now, it's like they're giving a speech. It's prepared. With him, it's just very conversational.

"But it's that personality, too. While I was growing up in New Orleans, all the musicians I played with had that personality. When I was younger and first got to New York, you'd meet guys and they just didn't have that. They'd be, like"—he put on a hippie voice—"'hey, how you doin', man, how's it goin'?' I'd be, like"—sharp, incredulous southern ratatat—"'*What the fuck is wrong wid y'all?*'

"And," he remembered evenly, "they'd say, 'You're an asshole.' I'd just never met people like that. But now . . ." He made an understanding face, raising his index finger to his brain and nodding. "They're from other places. They've got their thing."

We were listening to "Rockin' Chair" for the third time now. "That tempo," he exclaimed, "*no longer exists in jazz*. Find it. Who plays it? Nobody. That's the tempo that pulls your drawers down. That's what Art Blakey used to say."

That's the weird thing about going to hear Barry Harris, the old Detroit piano player, lead his band these days, I said. When Harris plays a bebop song with the tempo a little down, it feels so radical; it's like you're hearing it for the first time.

Marsalis agreed. Plus, he said, what people usually call the "complexity" of bebop—fast runs of notes in uneven clumps— plays to the strong suit of musicians who don't necessarily understand what they're playing. They can play it fast, but they're not making sense.

He mentioned that he had just been talking about this particular point with Joey Calderazzo, his quartet's pianist. (After Marsalis's move to Durham, Calderazzo relocated to Wake Forest, North Carolina, about an hour away. They talk on the phone all the time but don't see each other much, except when they're working.) "Joey used to say, 'I'm working on this bebop line,'" Marsalis explained. "He'd play it for me, and I'd say, 'That's not bebop.' He'd say, 'What do you mean *it's not bebop!*' So he went on this listening campaign for the last year, and he called me a few months ago, and said, 'A revelation just came to me. *Nobody* can play bebop. It's too hard. The stuff I used to call bebop really ain't bebop.' When you focus in on the notes—yes, they're bebop notes. But that's like saying the key to language is words. The key to language is not words; it's rhythm. It's all the little subtle things you can't teach: rhythm, tone, accents."

Marsalis talked about playing in an R & B cover band called the Creators as a teenager in New Orleans. "The job was to get people's booties wiggling," he explained, "and get them to dance. If it becomes too clinical, they won't."

The Creators prided themselves on what they considered brilliant segues: an Earth, Wind and Fire song, leading into the Eumir Deodato arrangement of the *Star Trek* theme, leading into a highly chromatic version of KC and the Sunshine Band's "Boogie Man." It didn't move the crowd, though. ("People would just sit there, bored as hell.") Meanwhile, the Creators were noticing another local band called Flashback, which had a drummer named Brick. Brick played with an overgrip, the stick enveloped by the fist, rather than the traditional jazz or drum-corps grip, the stick held like a pencil. And whenever Brick played the opening drumbeat of Stevie Wonder's "Superstition," people started dancing.

So the Creators got a new bass player and a new drummer. "And then," he explained, "we still did all that frilly stuff on the top, but now it was grooving, so people were cool with it. People don't *mind* the frilly stuff. They don't even pay attention to it. That's more for our personal edification. As long as it's grooving, everything's all right."

He put on a jazz analogue of the same story. It was "How Can You Face Me?" by Fats Waller, from 1934. It's pretty busy on the upper levels. Clarinet, guitar, and trumpet are adding lots of ornament; as Marsalis rightly pointed out, what they're doing isn't that special.

Waller, singing and playing piano, pours his personality all over the place. But the rhythm section stays steady; the bass notes (played by Billy Taylor) and the drum grooves (played by Harry Dial) are imposing, thick with volume and presence.

"Shit is swinging. *Chick-chick-chick-chick* . . ." He made a steady bouncing motion with his hand. "That's where the dance beat comes in. It's all about that. The other people just start launching off, but they just sit there and keep the beat." After Waller's opening piano solo, he starts to bust out over the other lukewarm soloists, yelling at the song's imaginary object: "Yass! Don't you *talk* back to me! Sheddup!" Marsalis beamed at that and started giggling. "As long as it's swinging, you can do that. I just love the fact that he's so exuberant, and so *foolish*."

Marsalis next wanted to talk about what he called authenticity. He meant the baseline truths of jazz: the cultural aspects of jazz — how it operated within a community of people, where they danced and in what patterns, how church and sex and money and race figured into a musician's life. (Though he took on parts of Coltrane's technical style early on, he says now that he didn't understand Coltrane very well until he was into his forties.) He finds himself listening to the basics of jazz very closely, the groove and the pulse and the aesthetic slang, rather than the speed and the harmonic acuity. Most of the jazz pieces he chose to listen to with me, in fact, had very slow tempos.

He put on Bessie Smith's "Need a Little Sugar in My Bowl," from 1931, where Smith is accompanied only by the pianist Clarence Williams. She sings it with concentration and force, almost simply. It's a sex song, and it is not coy. Only once does she

put a little English on a note, and between that and her connota-
tions, it's as if a little bomb were going off in slow motion.

> *I need a little sugar in my bowl,*
> *I need a little hot dog be-twee-ee-een my roll.*

"Whoo! Watch out, girl!" he whooped.

When Marsalis plays that song for students, he explained,
"they're, like, 'Where's the music?'" He picked up an alto saxophone, which he uses for practicing but never for performing, and
played the melody line very straight, with no swing. "No authenticity," he said. "I tell them, 'Man, you gotta growl, you gotta bend
the notes.'" He played it again with slurs and buzzes. "The way
most musicians are taught now relies on what they see, first, and
what they hear, second. They hear, but they don't hear. I want
them to learn this music and listen to it again and again. I'm forcing them to turn their ears on."

A few weeks before we talked, Marsalis had been visiting with
his wife's parents, outside of Malmö, Sweden. While he was there,
he heard some local swing musicians playing standards at a bar, and
he loved the fact that there appeared to be rules in their presentation. It was strictly 1930s and '40s repertory; the bass player slapped
the bass on every beat, *dang-dang-dang-dang*; and to solo for more
than one chorus was a sign of poor taste. ("I was just, like, *wow*," he
said, honestly impressed.) He asked to sit in, and they played "Up a
Lazy River," "Wabash Blues," and other songs he knew but doesn't
ever get to play. They asked Marsalis who he was, and he told them.
One of them recognized the name and said: "You play modern jazz.
I wouldn't have suspected you knew how to play this stuff."

He felt his generation was accurately sized up, and it made him regretful.

"Authenticity is out," he said. "I mean, look at this house, man. There's a hundred just like it. No. There's a *million* just like it, all over the country. When I first got to New York, it was clear to anybody that had been in New Orleans that I was from New Orleans, and it wasn't just from how I talked; it was from how I dressed. You know, dudes from Philly used to wear pointy shoes. They had pants with pleats, and they were kind of baggy. Now, man, everybody dresses the same."

His obsession with lieder has to do with the strength and cultural weight of the melodies—their authenticity, if you like. Another point in his long list of What's Wrong with Jazz Today is that young players tilt toward the standards with the most chord changes, which he believes often have the worst melodies. Recently a musician was arguing with him about the merits of modern big bands. Marsalis was saying that the new big bands don't have good enough melody; the other guy was saying that modern music has bigger fish to fry. "So I said, 'Modern music can't have melody?'" he recounted. "I said, 'Let me play you this.'"

He clicked on his copy of Stravinsky's *Ebony Concerto*, from 1946, as performed by the Ensemble Intercontemporain, conducted by Pierre Boulez. He has been wanting to record a new version of it, he said, with Larry Combs, the principal clarinetist in the Chicago Symphony who played a lot of jazz in an earlier life.

"See," he said, setting it up, "Aaron Copland writes a clarinet concerto for Woody Herman, and a couple of his guys studied with Stravinsky. So they said, 'Man, let's get Stravinsky to write something for Woody that would be a counter to it.' Stravinsky wrote it, and Woody's like, 'I can't play this shit.' So they used Woody's band, but they hired an outside clarinet player to play it. 'Cause that part is *sick*."

Ellington-influenced, and using a full saxophone section, *Ebony Concerto* has the order of melody Marsalis is looking for: not jazz-ballad melody, but something more relentlessly creative. ("It's modern as hell, and there's melody all through it," he said. "You can sing it all. That, to me, is what jazz at its best should be like.") More, it has one great idea after another for arrangement and instrumentation: acoustic guitar used beautifully, giant tonal shifts, passages that suggest Gil Evans's work fifteen years later. After one bit with muted trumpet and flutes—"*Sketches of Spain!*" he crowed—and then a long held note before a new section, Marsalis cheered. "*Igor!*"

What other classical pieces does your band have in its repertoire? I asked.

"None," he said, sounding impatient, as if he wished the answer were otherwise. "I wrote an arrangement of a Mahler piece that we haven't tackled yet. It's a piece from the *Kindertotenlieder*. It would be great, but it's on Joey to learn it. It's hard work, and he's doing other things, so I'm not blaming him."

Marsalis is so convinced that jazz has ignored classical music's resources that he sometimes sounds similar to those jazz players who are fighting the same battle on behalf of pop. But he believes that he's been through pop, and its riches can't compare. His ambitions, at least when we got together, were running miles ahead of the practical capabilities of his band—which says more about his ambitions than about what will certainly be seen as one of the best jazz groups of its time.

We spent a few minutes pinpointing parts of classical works that jazz composers may have stolen from. He mentioned Charlie Parker quoting Stravinsky—the opening bassoon line from *Rite of Spring*, which Parker used quite a bit—as well as a Sonny Rollins bootleg where Rollins quotes Rimsky-Korsakov's *Scheherazade*. And though it might have been a stretch, he was fascinated by the occurrence of John Coltrane's "Giant Steps" changes in Richard Strauss's *Der Rosenkavalier*.

This was all leading up to the fact that part of one of his pieces on *Braggtown*—a ballad called "Fate"—is borrowed from *Götterdämmerung*. "Straight-up Wagner, dude," he said. "I'm a student. I don't think of myself as this great inventor, so I don't mind giving up the truth."

It is a motif—usually called the "fate" motif—from right after the opera's overture; we listened to the version played by the Berlin Philharmonic and conducted by Herbert von Karajan. It is a slow, tense series of contrary-motion chords, played by woodwinds going up and brass going down. In Marsalis's tune, it becomes the first four notes of the opening theme; he plays it again right before Calderazzo's piano solo. "Once I realized where I got the melody from, I was like, who am I trying to fool?"

We listened to a long section, leading up to the theme in question. "I've never heard *Götterdämmerung* in concert," he said. "*Siegfried* and *Die Walküre*, yes, but this one's just so luscious. He used so many strings. Oh, man, it must be amazing, the sound of it."

Wagner-deficient, I was wondering if I'd missed it. I told him that he was going to have to signal me when the theme came in.

"I will," he promised. "I wouldn't do that to you, man." He chuckled.

A few minutes later he pointed to the crucial passage, about twelve seconds long. "Right there, that was it. When I was doing Leno's show, I'd come home and I'd listen to this every night, from beginning to end. I was by myself, so there wasn't nobody to talk to. I'd lay on the floor, because I didn't have a sofa. If there was a game on, I'd put it on and turn the volume down and listen to this.

"People thought I was strange," he remembered. "I might be."

Set List

Louis Armstrong, "Up a Lazy River," from *Fun with Bing and Louis* (Jasmine), recorded 1949.

Louis Armstrong, "Rockin' Chair," from *The Complete RCA Victor Recordings* (BMG/RCA), recorded 1947.

Fats Waller, "How Can You Face Me?" from *If You Got to Ask, You Ain't Got It!* (Bluebird/Legacy), recorded 1934.

Bessie Smith, "Need a Little Sugar in My Bowl," from *The Essential Bessie Smith* (Sony Legacy), recorded 1931.

Igor Stravinsky, *Ebony Concerto*, performed by the Ensemble Intercontemporain with Michel Arrignon, conducted by Pierre Boulez (Deutsche Grammophon), recorded 1981.

Richard Wagner, *Götterdämmerung*, conducted by Herbert von Karajan (Polygram), recorded 1969–70.

15

You Don't Look for Style

Guillermo Klein

In theory jazz is about constant reinvention. In practice it is full of references to its own back history, full of musicians working out small and precise variations on well-established languages.

Sometimes it's hard to find a new jazz group in New York that sounds as if it's aiming naively high, straining against its knowledge and its limitations, making music that produces the reaction *yes, of course; why hasn't that happened before?* Guillermo Klein's big band, for a few years, playing in tiny clubs around New York City, sounded that way.

Yet he didn't capitalize on the momentum that he was building in the late 1990s. He disappeared from town in 2000, moving to Argentina, his home country, and then to Barcelona, where he fit into a strong jazz scene and started a family.

New York City generally doesn't draw the short straw like this. During his subsequent evolution we heard dispatches from Klein—three fascinating records. Meanwhile, his music— in memory, mostly—worked like a secret code in the minds of young jazz players. Nothing else in town was filling the space it had occupied.

So when Guillermo Klein returned to New York with his band, Los Guachos, to the Village Vanguard in the summer of 2006, a number of people were unusually happy to see him again. I was one.

In early 1994, Klein, a pianist and composer, arrived in New York City from Boston, where he had attended the Berklee College of Music. He was twenty-four and soon found himself at Smalls, the Greenwich Village basement club on West Tenth Street that opened the same year. Most of the members of a seventeen-piece band he had been writing for in Boston came down when he got a gig at Smalls in December; in February 1995 he was given every Sunday night at the club and kept that schedule for four years, more or less.

"He had such trust in the musicians," the singer Luciana Souza remembered of those nights. "He would bring in a sketch, and sometimes the musicians would write their own parts, in the moment. Guillermo had an amazing pool of musicians, all soloists. Everyone was already a bandleader, and some of them already had record deals. But they were still in the spirit of this collective thing. It was like a troupe, a tribe."

His music resembled nothing else, especially as it moved toward grooves and away from the harmonic exercises he had learned in music school. It was jazz, of a kind, but it included brass choirs, counterpoint, drones, Argentine and Cuban rhythms, and a lot of singing. Some of the musicians were given parts to sing, and Klein sang himself, in a scratchy, smoky, untrained but emotional voice. There could be echoes of Steve Reich and Astor Piazzolla on the surface of the music; deeper inside, there might be clues to other heroes: Duke Ellington, Hermeto Pascoal, Milton Nascimento, Wayne Shorter, Stravinsky, and the Argentine pop composer Luis Alberto Spinetta. None of the admixtures sounded overthought, because Klein trusted his sense of song. If it didn't sound natural, he didn't play it.

And if the music directed too much attention his way, he reorganized it. Klein rarely takes a solo; I can't think of a more self-effacing bandleader who actually plays with his band on stage. (This rules out composers like Maria Schneider, who composes music for her own ensemble but only maneuvers a baton on stage.)

"I've written a lot of counterpoint," he told me in one conversation, "and I think I found it kind of by accident, as a way to play fugues. I was thinking, 'How do you deal with equality in sound? How do you make everybody equal?' Melody is amazing; it's the soul of the music. If I come up with a melody that I love singing, I don't want to chop it out. So, how can you make everything a melody?"

His colleagues and admirers came to include the best of their generation: Souza, Joshua Redman, Reid Anderson, Ethan Iverson, Mark Turner, Kurt Rosenwinkel, Tony Malaby, Jenny Scheinman, Claudia Acuña. Many of them were in his bands over the years; another six players from those days—Diego Urcola, Chris Cheek, Jeff Ballard, Ben Monder, Miguel Zenón, and Bill McHenry—have subsequently formed the American version of his eleven-piece group, Los Guachos (not Los Gauchos, as it has often been rendered in the English-language press). The word *guachos* is a common epithet in Argentina that can be used disparagingly or admiringly. Literally, it can mean "the orphans"; idiomatically, it means "the bastards."

There was an almost magical luck involved in the evolution of Klein's work, beginning with Smalls itself, which was unusual for its direct connection to the aspirations of young musicians. Klein's interest in self-promotion was dim at best. (It still is.) He was born in 1969. His parents weren't hippies, but he inherited from that era some of the best generalized hippie virtues. He has an instant dislike for art or personal exchanges that feel forced or mercenary. Asked when he knew he wanted to compose for a big band, this is what he said: "When you're young, you have more illusions. Then it's all just what it is. It's so much better. No expectations, just what it is and what comes your way. I don't think I will do a lot of things that I did before, like playing in restaurants. I don't think I will do it again. But maybe if I didn't have money.

"My music—it just happened. I started coming up with melodies, myself. I don't know. Playing my shit made me feel good, like I was sharing something. I felt at home with that. When I play this music, I feel nice. I feel honest and clear, a place to be."

During his six years in New York he didn't live on much; for the first two, his parents helped him. He and his musicians earned about fifty dollars a night at Smalls, although the opportunity to perform frequently with a big band—and to a growing audience—was lavish recompense.

He lived at a number of addresses in Manhattan and Brooklyn, including a Hell's Kitchen squat where he really did have to squat;

his bedroom ceiling was less than six feet high. He worked around a little bit. There was a spell as the pianist in Kurt Rosenwinkel's band at Smalls, and some time playing in a trio at the East Village bistro Jules.

For four months in 1997 he took a job in Chicago, playing in a Gipsy Kings cover band with an old friend from Argentina. In September 2000, missing home and not making much of a living, he and his American wife, the photographer and teacher Kim Bacon, moved to Buenos Aires.

I visited Klein, who was in his midthirties, one afternoon in November 2005 at his small apartment in the Eixample neighborhood of Barcelona, not far from Las Ramblas, the city's central boulevard. The night before, we had run into each other at a concert by his old friend Maria Schneider. Klein was worried, having second thoughts about having to express his ideas about music for a newspaper article. "I don't want to do any self-glorification," he said. I joked that I would do it for him, then. He looked even more worried.

Klein is happy to tell stories about himself and his friends, but when he starts feeling that someone may be tracing what might be called his career, he begins to worry. "If I get a hint that I am putting myself before the band, it feels bitter to me, it feels weird," he said. "I want the life of a simple guy, a simple musician."

During a long day stretching into evening, smoking cigarettes and listening to music, Klein talked about how he hears. He is self-effacing, honest, wary, calm, loyal, a gifted and sedentary bohemian, the kind of person that New York used to pride itself on nurturing, before hedge-fund managers restructured the supply-and-demand equation and turned Manhattan into

Venice. He spoke quietly, so as not to wake his one-year-old daughter, Veronica.

His father, also named Guillermo Klein, worked as a fruit vendor during Klein's childhood in Buenos Aires, then pushed his way to an economics degree; by the late 1980s he was president of Argentina's telephone company, in those days run by the state.

When Klein the younger turned eleven, his father gave him a piano. A year later Klein began composing; he started an apprenticeship with a teacher at fifteen, learning Bach fugues and chorales. His first pieces, he said, were inspired by Astor Piazzolla, the composer, national hero, and prime force of the *nuevo tango* movement.

What was the controversy about Piazzolla's music, to an Argentinian? "It's kind of like what happened with bebop, in the States," Klein said. "People stopped dancing, and some of the swingers resented it. He's the Monk, the Charlie Parker, the Mingus, the Dizzy, all together. Well, he was studying Stravinsky and Bartók; he studied with Nadia Boulanger, so he was using a lot of new harmonies from the start. He kept calling his music 'tango,' and a lot of people would say, 'Man, that's not tango.' And he would insist that it was.

"He went to study in France in the early fifties. He came back, he did an octet in '55. From then on, he was back and forth, out of Argentina, coming back," he said. "He had very wide recognition outside of Argentina. Very common, no? No man is a prophet in his own land. For example, he did this one song that made him very popular, called 'Balada Para Un Loco.' It's like a tango ballad, a pop tango. A lot of people reacted very negatively. They put it on a soap opera on TV, so you watch TV, you hear his music. We, the younger kids, didn't like tango. To a kid, it sounded cartoonish."

Like a caricature of the past?

"Exactly, *claro*. My father would listen to a tango, and he would get his eyes wet. I would listen to it at eight years old, and I would think it was funny.

"There are people that love Astor's fifties and sixties and seventies music," Klein explained. "But I love his very late work, from the eighties. I always listen as a composer. I need to hear the piece; I want to be inside the work. With this late period, his message was complete. I can hear it from beginning to end without wondering about form."

We heard "Contrabajísimo," a ten-minute piece from Piazzolla's record *Tango: Zero Hour*, which many consider his peak achievement. It was made with his New Tango Quintet, a band that was unusual for its jazz-trained musicians: the violinist Fernando Suarez Paz and the guitarist Horacio Malvicino. Typically for Piazzolla, it has a rugged theme, surging with conviction. (Piazzolla didn't engineer rhythmic flourishes into his music; his scores were written simply, and the players improvised conservatively but forcefully within them.) Then it grows soft and sentimental. "If you heard this section by a medium player," Klein pointed out, "it would be corny. It's flowery."

The piece returned to the aggressive main section. "Time goes by, and I cannot hear the chords," Klein said admiringly. "He makes you hear what he hears. It's so simple, the way it develops. Very obsessive. For me it's like an image of stepping very strongly along the earth and grabbing things, to go forward, clinging to them. Every step is really hard, taking you to a place that you didn't know you were going to reach."

The piece skidded to a stop. "Astor is like a friend that scolds you," Klein said. "He knows who you are, that kind of thing. If you write a good song, the first thing you think is, 'What would Astor think about this?'"

When Klein was eighteen, his father invited his piano teacher home for dinner, to ask whether it was practical for his son to pursue music. "The guy said, 'Yeah, definitely,'" Klein remembered. "'But he needs more than me. He should leave the country.'"

He had graduated from high school and played guitar in a rock band, covering Stones and Beatles songs. His mother read something in the newspaper about the Berklee College of Music; subsequently, the jazz vibraphonist Gary Burton, then a dean at Berklee, visited Buenos Aires to speak to music students. Klein attended the lecture and was struck by Burton's comment that performing with Astor Piazzolla was a high point in his musical life. Soon Klein was in Boston.

He loved Stravinsky, and his first thought was to study classical music. He knew very little about jazz, having heard it only by accident in shopping malls. He was under the impression that "Take the A Train" was a Rolling Stones song. (The Stones used a recorded version of the Ellington-Strayhorn tune as entrance music on their 1981 tour; Klein had seen the film made about the tour, *Let's Spend the Night Together*.) He had a poor command of English, and not much idea what he was doing in Boston.

"I showed the head of the classical department some fugues I had written, and he couldn't care less," he recalled, laughing.

"Then I met some guys, like Diego Urcola"—a trumpeter around his age, also from Buenos Aires—"who were talking with so much passion about jazz."

A month later he started listening to the Wayne Shorter record *Speak No Evil*, and something opened up. As a composer, Shorter is a genius of harmony in jazz; it is harder to parse his music in the scientific terms that music school can impose. Not very good at sight-reading and passionate about learning and composing by ear, Klein liked to find his way to voicings and harmonic motion that sounded as freshly discovered as possible; he sensed the same in Shorter.

Later, on holiday, he went to a Milton Nascimento concert in Argentina, which moved him to tears. He made his way to the mid-1970s collaboration between Shorter and Nascimento, *Native Dancer,* and he connected the dots between the two musicians.

We listened to "Miracle of the Fishes" from *Native Dancer*. It is a scary piece of music: first a brisk, three-beat figure on guitar, with descending harmonic movement, under Nascimento's tremulous voice, with a melody that sounds as if it starts from the middle. After fifteen seconds, everything begins to explode. An electric piano insinuates itself, and about two minutes in, Shorter appears, playing a great, gargly tenor-saxophone solo, slicing eccentrically phrased passageways through the chopping rhythm.

"I got very into this record," Klein said. "Maybe it was the fact of Milton and some grooves, also, which I felt close to, like kind of family." He made a few more passes at explaining his attraction to it, then gave up. "I don't know. The harmonies didn't feel like chords; they were like an orchestra.

"It felt good to be in there," he said, motioning toward the speakers. "It's very different to the tritone thing, I think."

This was another kick against music school. He was referring to the common substitute chords that are the basics of harmonic progression in jazz. Klein doesn't want to hear either hackneyed or overly fussy harmony. "I don't see the point," he complained. "A composer plays these voicings, writes down the names of the voicings, and then harmonically he has all these weird relationships. And then if you try to solo over that, you would never find it through the ears; instead, you find it through the eyes. E-flat seven sharp nine, going to A-minor seven flat five—how do you fit that through your ears, if it's just a voicing that you played on the piano? That's a very risky place, man. I hear that a lot, unfortunately. I get very bored."

I asked if his problem with a kind of official language of jazz harmony goes back to bebop. "No, no," he protested, "bebop is *incredible*. Charlie Parker is very clear to me. Bud Powell, too. They shape the harmony through the horn or through the piano, and you can hear exactly what harmony it needs. Bebop is one of the most important things in the twentieth century, and Stravinsky, you know."

He paused. "Secretly it has to do with the heart," he said. "How you feel in your heart. I bet Milton and everybody in that record was really moved, and they knew they were doing something really clear and honest."

He said that he and Reid Anderson, the American jazz bassist who spent some time living in Barcelona, had been talking about style and decided that it was all a construct. "You don't look for style," he said. "If something's going to be authentic, it will come out. I say, man, do your thing. What you're doing when you get with your friends—that thing becomes a style of its own.

"Like, we are filled with mediocrity, and some spots of inevitability," he continued. "When you hear Bach, you get the sensation that the whole thing was inevitable. It's an attempt to live every note. You feel part of something inevitable."

What might have been inevitable in 2000, when Klein and his wife relocated to Buenos Aires with five hundred dollars to tide them over, was the country's impending economic collapse. (His father, predicting the crisis, had warned him against moving back home.) He started to teach music and got a gig at a new club called Thelonious, where his band ended up playing every Wednesday night, eventually filling the club each week.

By the middle of 2001, the school where Klein taught wasn't issuing paychecks. By December, there was a freeze on bank withdrawals. On December 19 the band played a gig to about forty people at Thelonious, and when they finished, Klein was told by the owner that not one person had paid. The day after, there were riots in Buenos Aires.

"Nobody had any money," he said. "There was trading. People didn't have money to pay for lessons, so they would pay with food or a bicycle. You went walking everywhere. The thing is, there were people really listening at the club where we played, because it was such a crazy time that people needed to go out."

What came to Klein's rescue was a record deal with his American label, Sunnyside. In the middle of this mess, he made a record, *Una Nave*, which was finally released in 2005. It turned out to be a special record—one of the best of the year. In 2002 he moved to Barcelona, where he is finally making ends meet with regular local gigs and a teaching position in San Sebastián. Shortly after we spoke, he was finally given the honor of an invitation to play at the Vanguard, where he had never brought his band before.

For Klein's wedding in Begues, a mountain village south of Barcelona, some of his musician friends played an arrangement of the Billy Strayhorn song "Daydream," first recorded by Duke Ellington's orchestra in 1940.

We listened to the original version of the piece, not the slower, more tragic-sounding version recorded by the band shortly after Strayhorn's death in 1967. Klein wanted to demonstrate how one can come by jazz harmony honestly, rather than by following academic convention. What he zeroed in on was the bridge section of the song, where Johnny Hodges's throbbing alto saxophone works against Ellington's piano chords. "The changes are chromatic two-fives," he said—the ii-V module moving chromatically, half-step by half-step. "I had heard them before, like in some Charlie Parker blues, or in 'Darn That Dream.' But when I heard this, I didn't realize they were chromatic two-fives. I was so into the *song*.

"If you see the music on paper in the *Real Book*," he said—referring to the common cheat-sheet book of jazz standards that a musician might take to a pickup gig—"and you play the chords, this sounds like a typical jazz record. But if you hear the voicings they play, it's like, they are not chords. It's like a triad that goes to another triad, and the bass moves. It's just like a chorale, you know. See, an F-major chord, going to an F7 chord—it's like a can of soup. But if you do this voicing—A goes to G, E goes to E-flat, bass goes to C—you get all these new sounds. I mean, you can call it F7 if you want, but . . . the way they played that, it feels like they were discovering it. Like it wasn't done before.

"That's the thing about Duke; he makes the players *play*," Klein continued. "He makes them have fun. And he makes the writers write. I'm not a scholar of Duke at all; it's just that he brings me happiness. How could it be that you hear 'I Got It Bad and That Ain't Good' by everybody else, and it's okay, and then you hear it by Duke with Johnny Hodges playing and it's just, like *whoa*! It makes you fly; it makes you travel. I didn't read a lot about Duke, but I think he's my friend; I feel like he's my friend."

There are other stories to tell about Klein's horror of self-glorification. When Klein's *Una Nave* was released in the United States, for instance, it came with an unusual press release. "Guillermo Klein prefers that his music be judged without emphasis on biographical or historical context," it read. "Therefore, he has requested that a project biography not be written for the release of *Una Nave*. However, Guillermo did wish to relate that the music, recorded while living in Argentina, was passionately made and well rehearsed."

But he took to the project of listening and talking much the same way that the other musicians did, and more deeply than most. It suited his long attention span and brought out some long-standing feelings. Above all, he liked talking about how music moves through time, the mechanics that can make it seem, at best, unmechanical.

A year later, I saw Klein when he returned to play at the Vanguard again with his American band. He came upstairs between sets for a cigarette break outside the pizza parlor on the corner of

Waverly Place and told me that he had been thinking about things he wished we had listened to together: specifically, a song by Luis Alberto Spinetta, the Argentinian pop star, that gave him courage a long time ago. "He is my folklore," he said. I agreed that we could do it on the phone when he got back to Barcelona.

Like, for instance, Peter Gabriel, Spinetta started out as a fairly oddball artist before he became a mass-pop celebrity. He formed a band called Pescado Rabioso, which made three albums before he left; in 1972, he then made a solo album, *Artaud*, inspired by the French writer Antonin Artaud. It was credited to Pescado Rabioso, even though it was almost entirely Spinetta's own work.

Klein chose "Por," a short and beautiful voice-and-acoustic-guitar song from *Artaud*. There is a sense of ongoing discovery in this song. Its words are a series of images, each one separated by a comma: "arbol, oja, salto, luz, aproximación/mueble, lana, gusto, pie, té, marcas, miradas" (tree, eye, jump, light, approximation/furniture, wool, taste, foot, tea, prints, gazes).

"I remember that song specifically," Klein said. "Each word was like a little world for me. That was a strong thing for me—a sense of possibilities, but beyond thinking as a musician, just as a listener. Without thinking whether I would use it or not.

"A friend of mine was playing with him once, and he said that Spinetta would name each chord with people's names—like, for an A, he'd say, 'Play a Horacio chord.' He's very intuitive, very heavy. He came to see Los Guachos once, when we played in '98 in New York, at the Argentinian consulate. I saw him, and I couldn't avoid giving him a big hug. He told me that I was from Mars. I was like, wow, man. After *Artaud*, how can you say that to me? Maybe he meant from Mars, in some astrological sense. It was a deep day.

"He also encouraged me. I mean, I was talking to a musician, beyond the style. A true musician. He said that he liked the bridges of a couple of my songs. Tangible things. He liked 'Viva,' this very old song I wrote. Funny that he said that; when I wrote it, I thought of him. Harmonically free and very lyrical. It was my Spinetta moment."

Set List

Astor Piazzolla, "Contrabajísimo," from *Tango: Zero Hour* (Nonesuch), recorded 1986.

Wayne Shorter, "Miracle of the Fishes," from *Native Dancer* (Columbia), recorded 1974.

Duke Ellington, "Daydream," from *The Best of the Duke Ellington Centennial Edition* (RCA/BMG), recorded 1940.

Luis Alberto Spinetta/Pescado Rabioso, "Por," from *Artaud* (Sony/BMG Europe), recorded 1973.

Recommended Listening

The dates listed refer to when the music was recorded—that is, not the date of the album's original release or subsequent rerelease. All recordings will be found under the name of the musician in question, unless another bandleader's name is given.

WAYNE SHORTER

Introducing Wayne Shorter (1959, Vee Jay, rereleased by Koch). Under the spell of Coltrane, but playing his own phrases. With Lee Morgan on trumpet and the rhythm section of the late-1950s Miles Davis Quintet: the pianist Wynton Kelly, the bassist Paul Chambers, and the drummer Jimmy Cobb.

Juju (1964, Blue Note). The second in Shorter's remarkable string of records on Blue Note. Here the rhythm section is one of John Coltrane's: the pianist McCoy Tyner, the bassist Reggie Workman, and the drummer Elvin Jones.

Miles Davis, *Nefertiti* (1967, Columbia). Toward the end of Shorter's period with the Miles Davis Quintet, with some of Shorter's tersest and most brilliant writing: "Nefertiti," "Fall," "Pinocchio."

Native Dancer (1975, Columbia). A turnaround for jazz and for Brazilian music: Shorter's collaboration with the Brazilian singer Milton Nascimento.

Beyond the Sound Barrier (2005, Verve). A live recording of his great latter-day quartet.

PAT METHENY

Bright Size Life (1975, ECM). A language changer for jazz. With only three musicians: Metheny, the bassist Jaco Pastorius, and the drummer Bob Moses.

80/81 (1980, ECM). An inspired group. The bassist Charlie Haden and the saxophonist Dewey Redman come from Ornette Coleman's world; the saxophonist Michael Brecker was then known as a studio-pop session champion and still underrated as a jazz player; the drummer Jack DeJohnette was a freelancing rhythmic colorist, still yet to join Keith Jarrett's trio, the job that made him famous.

Rejoicing (1983, ECM). More laboratory experiments with Ornette Coleman's language, using the bassist Charlie Haden and the drummer Billy Higgins.

One Quiet Night (2001, Warner Brothers). A curious and beautiful strumming-heavy record for solo baritone guitar, recorded not long after 9/11.

The Way Up (2003–4, Nonesuch). A new challenge for Metheny, in long-form composition, and with an entirely different band.

SONNY ROLLINS

A Night at the Village Vanguard (1957, Blue Note). A fantastic trio, with the bassist Wilbur Ware and the drummer Elvin Jones. Sonny Rollins helped teach a generation of listeners to hear jazz in a new way. Compare his solos here to the best saxophone solos of a decade before—by Lester Young or Coleman Hawkins, say. These form perhaps a more detailed reflection of how the mind works: a record of everything an improviser is thinking, with gestures that might not necessarily lead anywhere but are still worth a try.

The Bridge (1962, RCA Victor). Rollins's return to music from the first of his long sabbaticals, full of stubborn and quicksilver logic. He sounds more himself than ever, and the contributions of the light-toned and self-effacing guitarist Jim Hall—a strange foil for a saxophone player with such a big sound—make the record deeper.

East Broadway Run Down (1966, Impulse). Trying to find his place anew in a jazz landscape that Coltrane had heavily imprinted, Rollins got together with Coltrane's bassist and drummer, Jimmy Garrison and Elvin Jones. (Freddie Hubbard plays trumpet on one of the three long tracks.) The record is full of hesitations and honest silences; it has a natural confidence, even sometimes the confidence to fail.

ANDREW HILL

Black Fire (1963, Blue Note). His first recording for Blue Note, from 1963, with the saxophonist Joe Henderson, the bassist Richard Davis, and the drummer Roy Haynes.

Point of Departure (1964, Blue Note). The most imposing of Hill's records, with whispers of jazz's past and future; with the trumpeter Kenny Dorham, the multireedist Eric Dolphy, the saxophonist Joe Henderson, Richard Davis, and the drummer Tony Williams.

Time Lines (2005, Blue Note). Hill's last album, his best in decades, with a cross-generational band.

ORNETTE COLEMAN

Complete Live at the Hillcrest Club (1958, Gambit). Once released under the pianist Paul Bley's name, these are live recordings of Coleman in a quintet with Bley, who understood exactly what Coleman was trying to do. The set is mostly Coleman's songs, although there is no Coleman on record that sounds closer to Charlie Parker. Knowing your jazz-history narratives, you might want to say they're at the edge of a great discovery, but in fact they're already waist-high in it.

The Shape of Jazz to Come (1959, Atlantic). The record that turned Coleman's fortunes around. Made in Los Angeles a few months before hitting New

York, it presents the great early Coleman quartet, with Don Cherry on cornet, Charlie Haden on bass, and Billy Higgins on drums. The record contains the uncharacteristically minor-key ballad "Lonely Woman."

Ornette! (1961, Atlantic). The end of the Atlantic period, still with Cherry but this time with Scott LaFaro on bass and Ed Blackwell on drums. The rhythmic connection between Coleman and Blackwell is the desired thing in jazz: flexible, coordinated motion.

The Complete Science Fiction Sessions (1971, Columbia). The tenor saxophonist Dewey Redman became a spur for Coleman, and he's part of what makes this early 1970s music special—that, and the realization of Coleman's song-like tunes as actual songs, with the singer Asha Puthli.

Sound Grammar (2005, Sound Grammar). A live recording by Coleman's recent band, in which his tendency to play high and speedily, floating his melodies (mostly new, except for "Turnaround" and "Song X"), is grounded by the low-end mass of two acoustic basses, bowed and plucked.

MARIA SCHNEIDER

Allegresse (2000, Enja). Schneider's big moment: when she lost interest in proving herself as a jazz composer with a system and a pedigree, and gained interest in writing what she liked most.

Cerulean Skies (2007, ArtistShare). When they start growing and changing after the first expositions of the melody, these pieces become extraordinary. This isn't small-band jazz with dressing; it is integrated and orchestral, a twenty-piece ensemble including accordion, *cajón,* and sometimes the singer Luciana Souza's wordless vocals.

BOB BROOKMEYER

Traditionalism Revisited (1957, Blue Note). A fresh look at the Dixieland repertory, sonically compact and emotionally rich.

Jimmy Giuffre Trio with Jim Hall and Bob Brookmeyer, *Western Suite*

(1958, WEA International). A lovely and radical record, airy and loose-sounding but largely through-composed, with folkish, cowboyish themes.

Stan Getz–Bob Brookmeyer, *Recorded Fall 1961* (1961, Verve). A casually virtuosic reunion of two improvisers who played together a great deal in the mid-1950s, in a quintet including Roy Haynes.

Gerry Mulligan, *The Complete Verve Gerry Mulligan Concert Band Sessions* (1960–62, Mosaic). A brilliant big-band project of the early 1960s, celebrated at the time but overshadowed in history by the contemporaneous free-jazz movement. Brookmeyer was cofounder, principal arranger, and, next to Mulligan, the prime soloist. (The album can only be ordered from mosaic.com.)

Clark Terry–Bob Brookmeyer Quintet, *Complete Studio Recordings* (1964–66, Lonehill). A warm, terrifically smart band from the mid-1960s, with Hank Jones and the drummer Osie Johnson in the rhythm section.

Spirit Music (2006, Artist Direct). The New Art Orchestra—Brookmeyer's largely European eighteen-piece band, with the American drummer John Hollenbeck—in a program of new music. It is his latest step in the evolution of modern, large-ensemble jazz writing that wound through Count Basie's 1950s music and the Thad Jones–Mel Lewis Jazz Orchestra of the 1960s.

DIANNE REEVES

In the Moment: Live in Concert (2000, Blue Note). Leading her audience through its paces, with many of her own songs, including the self-empowerment pieces "Testify" and "The First Five Chapters."

Good Night, and Good Luck (2005, Concord). Reeves in front of a small acoustic jazz band, singing old songs without losing herself to them.

BEBO VALDÉS

Mucho Sabor (late 1950s, Palladium). From the height of the 1950s mambo era in Cuba, Bebo Valdés and his band Orquesta Sabor de Cuba back up a number of the day's popular singers, including Pío Leyva and Orlando "Cascarita" Guerra.

Bebo and Cigala, *Lágrimas Negras* (2002, Calle 54). The collaboration that made him famous again: Valdés and the flamenco singer Diego El Cigala on a collection of old boleros.

Bebo de Cuba (2002, Calle 54). Recent music for a modern Latin-jazz big band, recorded with a wrecking crew of New York–based musicians including the saxophonists Paquito D'Rivera and Mario Rivera, the trombonist Papo Vázquez, the bassist John Benitez, and the drummer Dafnis Prieto.

Bebo (2004, Calle 54). A historically broad solo-piano recording, focusing on nineteenth- and early-twentieth-century Cuban music, *danzas*, and popular songs. Some of this music is little known and seldom played; Valdés performs it with elegance and feeling.

JOSHUA REDMAN

Spirit of the Moment: Live at the Village Vanguard (1995, Warner Brothers). The music sounds a bit old now, but this record is the summary of Redman's early working band, with Brian Blade on drums. Showy stuff, but it signaled a newly energetic kind of straightforward, acoustic jazz mainstream. You can tell why Redman became the next young jazz musician known to the Average Person. With a version of "St. Thomas."

Kurt Rosenwinkel, *Deep Song* (2005, Verve). Ten years later, and Redman's sound is still as clean and logical, but he's in Rosenwinkel's band, playing hard through oblique or more self-consciously naive music, alongside his old colleague Brad Mehldau.

Back East (2006, Nonesuch). The tenor-saxophone-trio format, for which Redman has the requisite flow. He's all grown up, engaging but never cloying, and his rhythm section cuts through the music with clever arrangements. If the beginning of the record points toward Sonny Rollins, his musical father, the end refers to (and includes) his actual father, the saxophonist Dewey Redman.

HANK JONES

The Talented Touch (1958, Okra-Tone). Jones was ubiquitous in the 1950s in a backline-for-hire with the guitarist Barry Galbraith, the bassist Milt Hinton, and the drummer Osie Johnson. (One of their records had the satisfying-harrumph title *The New York Rhythm Section,* at a time when there were many very good ones, though possibly none so widely recorded.) *The Talented Touch* rearranges standards like "My One and Only Love" and "It's Easy to Remember"; it is sturdy and clever, a handsome product of postwar American culture.

Steal Away (1995, Verve). Jones prides himself on taking instrumental challenges, so the gospel repertory wouldn't be an obvious way for him to go. But this record of duets with the bassist Charlie Haden was perhaps the first time in forty years that a Hank Jones record had been part of a contemporary current: an ongoing investigation by jazz musicians, including the singer Cassandra Wilson, the cornetist Olu Dara, and the pianists Eric Reed and Jason Moran, of gospel and blues and folk sources.

Joe Lovano, *I'm All for You* (2003, Blue Note). A ballad record, with Jones as a member of Joe Lovano's quartet. A balance is achieved, not just between the sensibilities of different generations—Lovano was born in 1952, Jones in 1918—but between Jones, with his high-1950s style of accompaniment and linear soloing in bop harmony, and Paul Motian, with his stark, shifting patterns in perfect time.

ROY HAYNES

Sarah Vaughan, *Swingin' Easy* (1954, Emarcy). Haynes up against Vaughan's swing and improvisational power in excelsis, from 1954, including the extra-slow "Lover Man."

Roy Haynes–Phineas Newborn–Paul Chambers, *We Three* (1958, OJC/Fantasy). Rugged but finely detailed straight-ahead jazz from 1958, including "Reflection," with Haynes's Latin-influenced high-hat rhythm.

Chick Corea, *Now He Sings, Now He Sobs* (1968, Blue Note). Corea's first album as leader. An uncanonized record in the wider world, yet most younger jazz musicians know it backward and forward.

Pat Metheny, *Question and Answer* (1989, Geffen). One of Metheny's few straightforward jazz records, rhythmically strong, with a trio including Roy Haynes and Dave Holland on bass.

The Roy Haynes Trio (1999, Verve). A self-portrait of Haynes's sound and history with an unfortunately short-lived band, including the pianist Danilo Pérez and the bassist John Patitucci.

PAUL MOTIAN

Bill Evans Trio, *Sunday at the Village Vanguard* (1961, Fantasy). The live sessions that helped rearrange small-group playing in jazz. The single CD may be all you need; it's also available as three unabridged CDs, with five different sets from the afternoon and evening of one day, called *The Complete Village Vanguard Recordings, 1961*.

Keith Jarrett Quartet, *Fort Yawuh* (1973, Impulse). From Jarrett's often-overlooked mid-1970s American quartet, with the saxophonist Dewey Redman and the bassist Charlie Haden, a band that set one of the great examples of freedom within structure.

Marilyn Crispell and Gary Peacock, *Nothing Ever Was, Anyway* (1997, ECM). The slowly unfolding, songful music of Annette Peacock, arranged for a quiet and powerful trio.

Paul Motian Trio, *On Broadway,* vol. 3 (1991, Winter & Winter). His long-standing trio with the guitarist Bill Frisell and the tenor saxophonist Joe Lovano, playing American-popular-songbook repertory live with the alto saxophonist Lee Konitz.

Paul Motian Band, *Garden of Eden* (2004, ECM). His three-guitar, two-saxophone band of young musicians, roaming around a few Charles Mingus tunes and a lot of originals.

BRANFORD MARSALIS

The Beautyful Ones Are Not Yet Born (1991, Columbia). Mostly a pianoless-trio record, and an accomplished one—if not as wild as what the trio would later play—with the bassist Robert Hurst and the drummer Jeff Watts. Wynton Marsalis comes in for a memorable tangle with the trio on one track, "Cain and Abel."

Requiem (1998, Columbia). The last recording of the old quartet, with the pianist Kenny Kirkland, who had been an important part of Marsalis's circle since the early 1980s. At the time it seemed almost the apotheosis of the jazz mainstream, sure-footed in its shifts of dynamics and tempo.

Eternal (2003, Marsalis Music). Here Marsalis evokes Ben Webster as much as Coltrane and performs a serious, sensual exploration of ballad tempos, many slower than normally heard in jazz.

Braggtown (2006, Marsalis Music). A quartet with an unmistakable new elasticity and cohesion, and an extreme range of expression, from serene ("O Solitude") to nearly violent ("Black Elk Speaks").

GUILLERMO KLEIN

Los Guachos II (1999, Sunnyside). Recorded before Klein left New York, this album is the American band at its best, with the singers Luciana Souza and Claudia Acuña, and two of Klein's near masterpieces, "Diario de Alina Reyes" and "Se Me Va La Voz."

Una Nave (2002, Sunnyside). Made in Buenos Aires, with a well-practiced Argentine band. Moments of something like rock, to Indian and Cuban rhythms and the Argentine *milonga,* powerful contrapuntal writing for brass, and a few of Klein's own original vocal performances.

Photography Credits

Grateful acknowledgment is made to the *New York Times* and the photographers:

Wayne Shorter by Cindy Karp

Pat Metheny by Jennifer S. Altman

Sonny Rollins and Andrew Hill by Eric Johnson

Ornette Coleman and Roy Haynes by Lee Friedlander

Maria Schneider by Joe Fornabaio

Bob Brookmeyer by Bob LaPree

Bebo Valdés by Francesco Sapienza

Dianne Reeves by Nan Melville

Joshua Redman by Jim Wilson

Hank Jones by Michael Kenneth Lopez

Paul Motian by Fred R. Conrad

Branford Marsalis by Jennifer Taylor

Guillermo Klein by C. J. Gunther

Acknowledgments

Thank you: Myra Forsberg, the editor who started running the original pieces; Jan Benzel, who continued them; Sam Sifton, who oversaw them; Jon Abbey, Sam Stephenson, Nat Chediak, and Lee Friedlander for scrutiny and company.

Index

Index

About the Author

BEN RATLIFF has been a jazz critic at *The New York Times* since 1996. The author of *Coltrane: The Story of a Sound* and *The New York Times Essential Library: Jazz,* he lives in Manhattan with his wife and two sons.